W9-CRR-300

COMMITMENT AS A THEME IN AFRICAN AMERICAN LITERATURE

A Study of James Baldwin
and
Ralph Ellison

R. Jothiprakash

Wyndham Hall Press

COMMITMENT AS A THEME IN
AFRICAN AMERICAN LITERATURE

A Study of James Baldwin and Ralph Ellison

by R. Jothiprakash

R. Jothiprakash, Ph.D. (Sri Venkateswara University), is a member
of the English Faculty of Deemed University (Gandhigram) and has
conducted major research in African American literature at both
Grambling State University and A and T University in North
Carolina.

Library of Congress Catalog Card Number

94-060406

International Standard Book Number

1-55605-237-5 (paper)
1-55605-239-1 (cloth)

Printed in the United States of America

Wyndham Hall Press
Bristol, IN   46507-9460

TABLE OF CONTENTS

PREFACE

The book entitled *Commitment as a Theme in African American Literature: A Study of James Baldwin and Ralph Ellison* represents an attempt to examine the nature of commitment in the works of James Baldwin and Ralph Ellison. This investigation involves an understanding of the social milieu against the background of the rapidly changing character of black fiction keeping pace with the complex development of the black American community in constant quest of a political and cultural identity. Haunted by the memories of "slavery, protest and fury, and the contradictory search for dignity in a world dominated by white values, the conflict between the artistic and political natures of the writer, his sexual complexities, the existential quality of his life, his need for an ethnic definition of himself", the black writer found his mission challenging. Richard Wright, who established that "The Negro is America's metaphor", gave the black American novel a place of its own in American literature. This thesis takes up the works of the two major black writers who succeeded him to examine the distinct individual methods adopted to serve the common cause. Equally deep in commitment to society, Baldwin and Ellison differed in perspectives and methods of execution. This book makes exhaustive analytical studies of their masterpieces against the background of complex political and ethnic configurations and the resultant political, social and psychological problems. It attempts to present an evaluation of their respective contributions which are the same in essentials but differ in details. References to other writers both black and white, are introduced at relevant places for purposes of comparison and contrast.

The book is divided into seven chapters. The introductory chapter entitled 'Commitment' offers various definitions of the term, and examines the connotations pertaining to literature. Positive as well as negative impacts of committed literature are examined in terms of the contribution it can make to society by voicing protest and inspiring action, thus engineering changes. Literary commitment can lead to the multiplication of works serving only as tools of propaganda, and can have adverse effect on aesthetic values. The black writer has, the chapter proceeds to explain, a double commitment: one to the mainstream of American culture of which he is a tributary, the other is to his own cultural identity as a black American. Baldwin and Ellison are to be interpreted from this perspective, and the manner in which their sacred pledge has been discharged to be analysed.

The second chapter is an exhaustive survey of the genesis and evolution of black literature in America. At the outset, it offers definitions and specific interpretation of the popular nomenclatures and epithets such as 'Negro', 'Black', 'Black American' and 'Afro-American'. Due references are made to the folklore and narrative tradition which exerted considerable influence over subsequent writers. It explains how the 'Harlem Renaissance' augured the inception of a 'third Force' on the American literary scene and played a pivotal role in the formation of a people's sensibility. The chapter highlights the important landmarks in the field. Starting with the accounts of problems confronting Negro slaves of African origin, the works gradually took on the tones of resistance, protest and revolutionary zeal. These voices differed widely. Adequate references are made in this context to famous books like *Uncle Tom's Cabin* written by a white novelist, Harriet Beecher Stowe. Another masterpiece examined in this chapter is Alex Haley's *Roots*, "the sprawling generational saga", a work of historical fiction and "a rich and weighty narrative about a black House whose origination antedated the nation itself". Haley, a 'hybrid', voices the realisation of the black American that he owes allegiance both to his American present and the African origin. The chapter refers to several other writers such as Paul Dunbar, Claude McKay and Langston Hughes.

Richard Wright's epoch-making *Native Son* is introduced at this point. The 'great thrilling shiver of delight' caused by this novel, has had a very strong impact on the black sensibility as well as on the general public. His works created certain unwelcome repercussions too. Yet, Wright's commitment was strong and his message was clear. It was caught by the succeeding generation who took the spirit even while slackening the dissent and regulating it into wholesome directions.

The subsequent chapters offer analyses of the individual works of James Baldwin and Ralph Ellison, two chapters each being devoted to the study of an author. *The minor reversal of the chronological order that of considering Baldwin first in spite of his having been younger than Ellison, is followed here taking into account the fact that unlike Baldwin who is no more, Ellison continues to be a vibrant living force today.* Whereas Wright engages in fantasies of rage and violence against whites for casting him out, Baldwin commits himself to pursue another path to self-respect -- persuasion and love. Baldwin, trained as a pulpit orator, had immense faith in the efficacy of words, and therefore the depth of his commitment was expressed through the powerful medium of compelling statements and convictions. His masterpieces both fiction and non-fiction are analysed. Some of his essays echo a crescendo of anger, reflecting his own perplexity, struggling to establish the correct social relations as well as an identity of his own. His attempt was to achieve a kind of permanent truce between his African and American selves. Baldwin's agony at this painful quest is reflected in his works, thereby making him a symbol of such a commitment. This aspect has enriched his art. In general, these two chapters attempt to establish Baldwin's right to be considered as the spiritual chronicler of his age.

Ralph Ellison, equally deep in commitment to his race, has succeeded in raising his *Invisible Man*, an established classic of modern American literature to the level of a metaphor, not only of his own self or that of the blacks in America, but even that of historical situation. The nameless hero of the novel moves "from invisibility to vision". It deals not with history alone, but with black experience and human soul on the whole. The chapters relating to Ellison's works point out the unique individual characteristic of his art which converted invisibility into a kind of allegory giving it a concrete personality. Ellison wanted not only to *be heard* as Baldwin did, but was meant to *be seen* to create a strong visual impact and to make the unseen manifest. Invisibility, for him, meant his loss of self.

These four chapters have attempted to point out the individual differences in the perspective of the two committed masters of the literary medium. Protest, resentment, revolution and reconciliation -all these varying moods are reflected in the worlds of these thinkers. Committed to the demands of a changing society, they wanted to give it a healthy, positive direction. Both Baldwin and Ellison endorse the assertion of Dr. Martin Luther King Jr. that "An eye for an eye policy will ultimately leave both blacks and whites blind". This point is substantiated by abundant references to the texts.

The concluding chapter makes an attempt at a balanced reassessment of the contributions of Baldwin and Ellison. It takes up the major points of criticism levelled against their art, concerning the themes or the technique. Special attention is paid to the views of critics who question the validity of their contribution to society as genuine spokesmen of the blacks in America. One such attack levelled is that both the writers had failed in their mission pioneered and upheld by Richard Wright. This chapter offers to handle such criticism by examining them in the due context. Taking the protagonists in their major works as the metaphors reflecting their approach, the study analyses the writer's stance on political and social issues specifically applicable to the blacks in America. Another point examined in the final chapter is the nature of their political affinity, drawing the conclusion that both Baldwin and Ellison had drawn inspiration from Marxist ideology, but in terms of direct involvement with the Communist Party the influence can be brought down to the minimum. An important issue, treated from two angles deals with influences, mainly of a literary nature, on their works as well as that which the succeeding generation of writers has drawn from them. The book

v

closes raising a plea for further investigations into the remarkable contributions of Baldwin and Ellison.

I am very grateful to Dr.(Mrs.) Radhamani Gopalakrishnan, my Research Supervisor for her guidance and encouragement. She has been a great source of inspiration to me in the successful completion of this book. I am also thankful to Dr. G. Nageswara Rao, Dean of the Faculty of Arts and Dr. T. Krishna Rao, Head of the Department of English, for their timely help and support during the period of my research. I record my sincere gratitude to Dr. K. Mahadevan and Dr. S. Gopalakrishnan for their genuine interest in the progress of my work.

Giving adequate expression of my indebtedness to Dr. Francis Abraham and Ms Subhadra Abraham is rather a difficult task. My visit to the Grambling State University, U.S.A., was possible only because of their goodwill and generosity. Let me express my thanks to the President, Librarian, Dr. V. T. Samuel, Prof. Achuthan, Dr. Ramamoorthi, Dr. Joseph Kurian, Mr. Eddie Cook and Ms Deborah Stevens of the Grambling State University for their support in carrying out my research work. I am much beholden to Dr. Margaret Walker Alexander, a well-known writer and close associate of Richard Wright for her informal interview with me on black American literature and to Dr. Frances Staten for having arranged the meeting with the writer. I owe a debt of gratitude to Dr. Barbara Dicks of the University of Connecticut, Mr. Dennis A. Almeida of Rhode Island and Ms Mary Shettig of Florida for sending me the books and other material for my study as and when I needed them.

I am indebted to the American Studies Research Centre, Hyderabad and the Librarian and the staff of Sri Venkateswara University Library for assisting me in my data collection.

I am thankful to my colleagues in the Faculty of English, Gandhigram Rural University and to other friends including Dr. P. Bayappa

Reddy of Ananthapur, Prof. V. S. Ramani of Madurai, Prof. V. Mani of Tiruchy and Prof. H. G. Kulkarni of the University of Pune for their timely help and useful suggestions. I would like to thank Mr. E. Ekambaram, S. V. University, Tirupati for his assistance in this connection.

I owe a special debt of gratitude to the members of my family for their loving care and concern throughout the period of my research work.

R. Jothiprakash

INTRODUCTORY NOTE ON THE TEXT

The titles of the following books have been abbreviated and parenthesized in the text:-

TITLE OF THE BOOK	ABBREVIATION
1. *Go Tell It on the Mountain*	*Go Tell*
2. *Notes of a Native Son*	*N.N.S.*
3. *Nobody Knows My Name*	*N.K.M.N.*
4. *The Fire Next Time*	*T.F.N.T.*
5. *The Price of the Ticket*	*The Price*
6. *Blues for Mister Charlie*	*B.C.*
7. *Invisible Man*	*I.M.*
8. *Shadow and Act*	*S.A.*
9. *Going to the Territory*	*G.T.*

CHAPTER ONE

COMMITMENT

Literature is by its very nature a social art committed to human values. Its role as a potent medium of communication entails more of responsibility than privilege to the writer. It carries a great deal of social significance especially when it is committed to politics—not the politics of right and left, but the politics of right and wrong—to the humanistic gestures and to artistic principles. The image of the writer as an idle singer in the ivory tower and a vendor of illusions is no more tenable in the modern context. The publication of a work is essentially an act of communication through which the writer seeks to impose his personality and vision of life on the society. Commitment stands for the basic cast of mind, the genuine devotion of the writer to a cause and his convictions. It denotes a pledge, an involvement of the nature of a binding promise, implying a clear stand in a specific problem arising out of a deep consciousness of the various dimensions of the issues concerned. "A committed or *engagé* writer is one who through his work, is dedicated to the advocacy of certain beliefs and programs especially those which are political or ideological and in aid of social reform."[1] *The Oxford English Dictionary* defines the term commitment as an engagement that restricts freedom of action. This is not as negative as it sounds. It indicates an ideology firmly held and a perspective adhered to with zeal and dedication. The intensity of the commitment arises from the sense of moral fervour and righteousness. Conviction goes with commitment. It can include the willingness to work for a well-defined ideology aimed at the reform that the writer has in mind, and the dissemination of the faith.

Commitment "is an awareness, an attitude, a clear and feelingful recognition of being fully present in the moment, making the choice of the moment, and standing by the consequences of these choices whether anticipated or not."[2]

In a spectacular semantic explosion the word "Commitment" has gathered to itself an astounding variety of new meanings.

An examination of contemporary criticism reveals that the word, and its various adjectival forms have recently assumed new literary connotations. It has emerged as one of the most frequently used literary terms. It has raised a number of literary problems and the writers have passionately chosen sides on the problem.

Writers do not live in a vacuum. They are sensitive to the world around them more acutely than others. So their works bear the impact of their times. Yet, reflecting the deepest mood of their times, the writers shall also shape their times. Thus they are shaped by their age and they mould their age, too.

In an epoch of intense social transformation political and social forces exert considerable influence upon the artists, responsive to these forces. The forms of commitment and the political alternatives chosen by writers living in an age of controversy differ. The aesthetic consequences of their choices form a distinctive aspect of the study of literature. Thus the term commitment includes "both the conscious *involvement* of the artist in the social and political issues of his age (in contrast to deliberate detachment or political noninvolvement), and the specific political *obligations* which the artist assumes in conse-quence of this involvement..."[3] Analysis of the evils in society leads to violent disapproval and protest. Registering this protest has become one of the major functions of literature. The writer by his very nature cannot help being conscious of vital political issues. Thus it is clear that commitment is conceived as a social and political activity. The writer must commit himself to the political arena in order to retain his integrity as an artist.

Thus the term commitment is used as an equivalent to an undertaking or an obligation. It includes any belief which incurs obligation whether individual or social. The writer commits himself to work for an *individual,* an *ideology* or an *institution.*[4] His belief may include non-political areas such as moral, religious or aesthetic and their literary consequences. Since the implications of commitment are greatly widened, it is not possible to speak of the act of commitment without predicating an object to which the writer is committed. The question which inevitably arises is what he is committed to. All art is committed to human as well as aesthetic values. Insofar as the artist is concerned with aesthetic commitments, there is no problem. The problem arises when he is committed to values or actions extrinsic to the immediate concerns of his art, i.e., when he is forced by non-aesthetic considerations such as political, social or religious commitments. If the writer is committed to certain social objectives, he is invariably involved with considerations of means to realize them. The effect of a writer's commitment on his work has to be judged in the light of the purely literary or artistic merit of his work. Only then can it be decided whether his commitment has vitiated the artistic integrity of his work and degraded art into propaganda. Time is the arbiter of this. If the work retains life and significance long after the resolution of the issue that gave rise to it, it may be concluded that his art has transcended contingencies of propaganda.

Therefore, it is imperative and justifiable that a writer must be committed to the promotion of human values. There are certain fundamentals of human decency which must be preserved and protected. But it would be absurd to deny that there are occasions when aesthetic standards and our central human values clash. His affiliation to certain doctrines and actions may adversely affect the aesthetic value of his work. The importance of political commitment as a literary problem engenders a number of aesthetic dilemmas.

Political commitment involves two pertinent problems: the moral problem examines whether the artist as a human being living within a social situation which demands political resolution can evade these problems in his art and still retain his integrity as a social being and the aesthetic problem raises the question if the artist can evade these problems in his art and still maintain the integrity of the work. The concept of commitment has thus emerged as a subject of debate. At bottom, it is a question of discharging one's responsibility without fear or favour and it is essential for the artist. Kenneth Tynan in his essay, "Theatre and Living" argues that "if all art is a gesture against death... it must commit itself".[5] His argument is assertive and in a clear positive tone indicating the creative role literature has to play in society. He points out that there are three attitudes toward life open to the writer: he can record it imitatively; he can withdraw from it; or he can seek to change it. He is of the opinion that great art must do more than record details; it must comment. Literature demands, besides interpretation, resolution as well. Therefore, the artist is expected to involve himself with social questions, to immerse himself in the milieu of which he is an integral part. Art which evades social issues is like a flower that "is born to blush unseen" and "waste its sweetness on the desert air."[6] The other pole of this argument is that the artist should not lose himself in his times.

The liabilities of the political commitment of writers must not be overlooked. Some writers have become loath to involve themselves politically as they find their writings discounted or discredited as a result of their 'position taking'. For example, as a response to a question about the artist's relationship to the growing tension between the Soviet Union and the United States: "Do you think a writer should involve himself in it (as writer, as person)to the point of commitment?" several writers affirmed the writer's detachment. Clement Greenberg "asserted that while the *person* might have political obligations the writer had obligations only to his art," Leslie Fiedler also declared that "although the writer may at times be forced into a position of political commitment, he is so at the sacrifice of his role as a writer" and Rosenberg opined: "there is an inherent conflict between artistic integrity and any commitment."[7]

The significance of political commitment for the artists and the consequences of their conscious involvement in the social issues of the age in which they live are, by no means, a simple problem. Writers when they confront such problems may keep quiet on things going wrong or convert a concrete crime into an abstraction and tell the ruling class what it wants to hear.

In some extreme cases, especially in the totalitarian regimes, the writer is compelled not only to be socially alive but also more openly to join the common people in their struggles. He cannot afford to have a neutral stance.

Such an *engaged* writer is expected to be a model to others and display his fidelity to the rulers, absorbing their outlook and speaking on their behalf in order to uproot dissent, to implant favourable ideas and to transform the conditions of life as designed by the rulers. The writer adopts the perspective of the rulers by parroting platitudes and converts himself into an *encaged* writer.

A major question raised in this context would be whether commitment represents a political assault on the integrity of the artists. It is looked upon at times as a leftwing plot to deprive him of his freedom, to make him follow certain doctrines, to forbid him from others and to force him to have no other God besides the leader of a particular cult or creed. It can, from the same perspective, be a ruse to impose on the artist new fetters or to clip his wings and keep him tied to a spot. A crucial issue is if it is a moral question that binds the artist and demands his allegiance to a specific cause. Further it raises the doubt whether it is a question to be asked of an artist's work rather than his life and whether the words on the page can be conceived as a self-sufficient entity.

These questions require careful consideration if the idea of commitment is thought of as useful, important and inevitable. There is, of course, something to be said on both sides of the argument. Since the term commitment is frequently referred to without much reflection it remains a nebulous concept.

"Writers were persecuted and killed precisely because literature was recognized as an important and potentially dangerous force."[8] Politics is seen, in the final analysis, as an instrument of oppression, no matter who wields it. The fear of politics lurks in the minds of writers.

Professionals like doctors and lawyers take a vow to follow their professional ethics and etiquette; politicians openly declare to abide by the constitution and religious heads commit themselves to God, the holy scriptures and the religious order. But writers have no such compulsion to commit themselves to anything. It is precisely this freedom that imposes tremendous responsibility on the writers.

The artist is committed to freedom by the very exercise of his art. Practical observation suggests that writers have bartered the freedom of their profession for power, pelf, position and at times, for mutually contradictory philosophies.

All art is committed, it would seem, to something beyond itself, to a statement of value, not purely aesthetic but to a criticism of life. There is no criticism of life that does not have social and political overtones. Whether a writer actually joins a party or embraces a creed or emulates a leader is of merely biographical interest.

> [The] biographical fact that Brecht never became a member of the Communist Party does not help us decide the important and difficult question of how far Brecht realized his "Marxist ideology" in his dramatic work. Brecht's commitment, like that of any other artist, must be sought in the work itself, not in Brecht's views about his own works.[9]

The writer can make his stand known without advocating it openly. Perhaps it is a measure of a writer's success when he can move people and pleasurably teach them without any offensive propaganda. "The function of art was to teach and educate and move and unify and organize people, not to mystify them or offer dazzling support of the status quo."[10] Therefore, a writer need not fight shy of propaganda.

It may be germane to ask if, when an artist is made a political propagandist, art is not sacrificed for politics or made subservient to it. The artistic function is not viewed as something separate from the political function, canceling or contradicting each other. The two functions do happily mix and blend, work together in harmony, support and strengthen each other. "Propaganda in some form or other lurks in every book, that every work of art has a meaning and purpose—a political, social and religious purpose—that our aesthetic judgements are always coloured by our prejudices and beliefs."[11] The novels such as *Animal Farm* and *Nineteen Eighty-Four*, written by Orwell, in spite of their obvious propaganda, have stood the test of time owing to the fact that the political situations dealt within these works still exist today. Commitment need not give rise to propaganda. It is not that propaganda is not necessarily a mistake; everything depends on the writer's vision and the manner in which he makes out his case. Therefore, it is pertinent for a society to ask of a writer to what he is, in the last resort, committed.

The expression social commitment is used in preference to the more familiar political commitment, since the former is more comprehensive than the latter. In fact, social commitment includes political commitment as well. The maladies affecting any society are more than simple questions of political programs or affiliation to political ideologies. If it is committed to social objectives of vital importance, literature has a wider relevance to modern society as it deals not only with political questions but with issues that lie beyond. Social commitment comprises all the aspects of involvement, and is thus wider in connotation.

Social commitment has three major aspects, the first being a deep and probing enquiry into the drawbacks of society leading to the sincere understanding of the problem, the second, considering and suggesting the possible remedial measures for all ailments of society, and the third indicating methods of implementing the solutions. Committed art thus becomes art with a clear social function.

Committed literature is bound to be basically subjective, reflecting the author's stand regarding major social questions. It would quite conspicuously represent the ardour of the writer's commitment to society. He does not seek freedom from the bondage: it is a pledge he has made of his own, not out of frustration or coercion, but out of the conviction that society can be improved, provided there is a concerted effort of the artist, of the social reformer, and, at times, of the politician as well.

The writer finds in life distortions which are repugnant to him, and his intention is to make these appear as distortions to his people who are used to seeing them as natural and he is forced to take all available means to get his vision across to the people. To the hard of hearing he shouts and for the visually impaired he draws large and startling figures. The people will take what he shows as a revelation. The committed writer has the sharpest eye for the grotesque and the perverse. He has the courage to call a spade a spade. He also shows the means to correct the distortions and to remedy the situation by calling attention to the fatal eventuality of frenzied action and the equally fatal consequences of apathy.

The writer, as a consequence of his commitment, may display a creative approach in his suggestions for positive reforms. Or he may be negative and destructive and emphasize violent disapproval and protest.

Literature thus embodies the ruthless scrutiny and criticism of social evils, dethroning and destroying all the undesirable values. Yet, creating positive faith in the human possibility for improvement and reform is an equally important and integral aspect of the socially committed art. Social reconstruction might be through different means. Political affiliation or collective political action might become necessary. Solutions might even be sought elsewhere. The specific method of achieving the purpose is secondary to the main issues. Political commitment is, thus, only one of the aspects of social commitment.

Once the writer is committed to a particular ideology he embarks upon a course of action to achieve his cherished goal. This leads to an examination of the relationship between art and commitment, trying to answer as to how far aesthetic values would suffer if the writer was a committed artist.

The Marxist "Agit-Prop" and the "Living Newspaper", produced in large numbers in the 1930's were meant to confront the audience directly with specific burning social problems and to suggest probable alternatives to solve them. These represented attempts to channelise the general mood of protest into specific directions. They were not aimed at producing wholesome works of literature with high aesthetic standards. Yet, though they were concerned only with the highlighting of certain issue, they were just a plain record of contemporary events.

These Agit-Prop and Living Newspaper forms of dramatic presentation cannot claim aesthetic or literary value. They are only tracts meant to serve specific purposes through propaganda, invective and suggestion. Yet, they succeeded not by aesthetic appeal, but by the portrayal of specimens of suffering humanity, thereby in establishing rapport with the audience, arousing a deep sense of social consciousness and rousing them to collective action, which may be even political in certain cases. They were meant only to create a sudden, though temporary, jolt among the smug, complacent people.

Even though the plays produced by Clifford Odets (1906-1963) were basically agit-prop in design, his overt commitment to the Marxist ideology has not affected the artistic integrity of his plays. His play *Waiting for Lefty*, (1935) based on the New York City taxi strike of 1934 was intended "to invite the audience to join in the final call for a strike."[12] In the play a group of workers are seen waiting for the arrival of their spokesman Lefty. A man enters and informs his comrades that Lefty has just been found, behind the car barns, with a bullet in his head. It is not the actors on the stage, but the entire audience who shout louder and louder still, "Strike". The play ends with the lyrical proclamation of the revolution. The audience and the actors are at once with each other. This proves how the playwright has succeeded in presenting the emotional values in all their poignancy, unimpaired by his party affiliation.

The committed writers like Clifford Odets have made substantial contribution to art and have produced literary works whose aesthetic value did not wane in spite of the overtones of extra-literary considerations. They had clear social perspectives, and even brief periods of political affiliations, yet their commitment to society never affected the intrinsic aesthetic standards of their works.

W. H. Auden, along with the other revolutionary poets of the 1930's, offers the best example of literary commitment. W. H. Auden had a clear Marxist affinity in the beginning, but soon outgrew it, and his later poetry reflects this change.

In his youth, even though he was committed to the clear political ideology in the efficacy of which he had deep faith, Auden's poetry included more than issues which simple political reforms could cure. He was conscious of psychological, religious and moral issues. Auden's formal commitment to the Communist Party was very brief, but his subsequent literary output shows that his social commitment never weakened. The edge of the Marxist ardour got blunted, but his consciousness and his commitment to the social problems never slackened.

There is in Auden's later poetry a general tone of reassurance in society. The ruins of social decay are highlighted by the testimony of the senses; and it is not surprising that the worlds of art and ideas should themselves be characterized by the search for social enlightenment. The pose of non-commitment, Auden came to feel, was itself a political act.

Literature is committed to the details of known experiences. The major tradition of European fiction which aimed at the delineation of the known experiences is described as realism. It emphasized the rendering in art, with precision and vividness, of the everyday, ordinary, contemporary reality. Attention was bestowed on the selection of material which was normally ignored or evaded and considered sordid, offensive or repulsive. Realism was thus the outcome of an appeal to the obvious truth of the visible external world and owed its sustenance to the disciplined principles of sciences.

If the descriptive function of the author is the shaping priority, the work is called documentary. On the other hand if a pattern taken from contemporary society is materialized as a whole and presented with improvement in another time or place it is called utopia. Utopia is speculative and enshrines a search for the best possible form of social order.

A third type of realistic fiction known as Science fiction includes predictable and probable projections based on fancy or fantasy and scientific experiments and inferences. Here the writer is concerned with the probable, not merely the possible, spectacular changes in the world, and with a blueprint for the future or nightmare visions of the unborn and avoidable future. There is yet another type of realistic fiction called the fiction of special pleading advocating a specific ideology or propagating a particular doctrine.

Thus realism has a wide connotation. It is not just a mechanical reproduction of contemporary reality. It is a recording process and yet a deviation is always possible based on the commitments of the writer and the needs and aspirations of society. It involves more than mere perception. New ways of perception, interpretation and organisation are possible and deeply necessary.

The emphasis is on truthful representation of external realities, but the creative talent of the artist can synthesize disjoint truthful aspects effectively. A scientific vision can arrange them into a clear, purposeful and logical pattern. Thus, the stress on truth carries realism far above the level of photographic realism generally used in a derogatory sense. The objectivity of realism "is not a dispassionate noninvolvement but a commitment to a particular reading of human society...."[13]

Realism as the conscience of literature confesses that it owes a duty, some kind of reparation, to the real world—a real world to which it submits itself. Thus conceiving of reality in a certain way, and presenting it, refer to the role played by creative energy in sorting out casually observed facts, arranging them in a particular order, and infusing the chosen facts, in short, with perennial literary value. *Reproducing* reality is different from *producing* reality; as the former involves the function of the critical and creative faculty which has to do both selection and elimination before presenting the finished product, whereas the latter is simply photographic in execution. The writer has a conscience to obey, and a duty to perform. Therefore he has to abandon the subjective line and depict life truthfully. His aim is truth—unconditional and honest.

The representation of material reality or visual realism later developed into the "investigation of the moral behaviour of man in society,"[14] where "character is a product of social factors and environment."[15]

Eric Bentley's comment "an increasing closeness to objective facts; special techniques for their reproduction; an empiricist outlook—these are realism... and it aims at the candid presentation of the natural world"[16] may be applied to all forms of literature produced by committed writers.   At the *primary* level realism busies itself with *depicting the life of common people,* reproducing their speech pattern and life style faithfully.   At the *secondary* level realism takes us into the *problems of contemporary* life of ordinary people whose responses to the demands of life constitute the basis of a neatly formulated pattern.   At the tertiary level realism leads into Zola's territory of *naturalism.* It denotes scientific objectivity in literary portrayals and represents empirical work.   It is an antithesis to idealism stressing the effects of heredity.

In the works of such writers a deeper and more acute understanding of the middle class life—its milieu and ethos-- is found and a genuine attempt is made to express social problems and to portray real characters.

Committed literature depicts the attitudes of an author who brings out realistic works with the consciousness of his function in society as a writer.   The power that is latent in each work of art should assert itself, and generate the necessary will-power with which social and political reforms can be effected.   The author's idealism is manifest in the zeal for reform that underlies a literary work.

Social Realism is very rarely used as an expression in critical terminology, except in the general or loose sense of literature that attempts realistic interpretations of the conflicts and problems inherent in modern society.   Social Realism is a phase in the evolution of realism, closely allied to the scientific interpretation of social history.   A work of fiction should reflect a certain phase in the social or moral history of the age.   With acute fidelity to the concrete facts of the external world, and the scientific approach, the expression Social Realism becomes self-explanatory.

The same instinct that impels the writer to expose the painful and sordid realities in society manifests itself in the form of Social Realism. Works of social realism need not necessarily have any political affiliation. Practical reform may be yet far off from the writer's field of vision.

Socialist Realism indicates the writer's commitment to the cause of society, and his determination to plan his role as an intellectual leader, in exposing the drawbacks through his writing and stating appropriate steps that are conducive to change. Socialist Realism, obviously, belongs to the modern age and it needs "an ideological correlate which is of primary importance", and is "written in the historical interests of the working class".[17] This alters realism from its sense of the direct reproduction of observed reality; realism instead, becomes a principle and organized selection. Thus, a proper blend of the subjective and the objective interpretation is expected of a committed writer. A statement made by Lukács makes this meaning clear, "... a correct aesthetic understanding of social and historical reality is the precondition of realism", and his prediction, "Society will eventually achieve a condition which only socialist realism can adequately describe."[18]

In a literary portrayal that is truly realistic, the element of social criticism along with suggestions of how the present could be improved is bound to be incorporated. The zeal for reform, even when presented indirectly, gives the work that idealistic touch. "Its life issues not from the autonomous character of the work but from the mutual interaction of work and humanity. Its life is founded in ... the 'life' of mankind ...."[19] It is this mutual interaction of work and humanity that forms the core of any literary work based on social awareness.

Bernard Shaw's definition of Problem Plays as "the presentation in parable of the conflict between Man's will and his environment,[20] may be applied to all committed literature. "Every serious play ends with a note of interrogation".[21] This is a correct statement not only of dramas but also of all committed writings because they do not and cannot give a satisfactory solution to the main questions posed, nor can any ending be totally satisfactory. Alternative solutions and alternative endings, in fact, entirely different handling of the theme itself, can be very frequently suggested. They are committed to the exposition of truth; several complicated situations in modern society are open to different interpretations and suggestions for improvement. At times solutions suggested by the writers may not be fully acceptable.

The writings leave scope for different ethical interpretations and alternative solutions. Often the problem raised remains unsolved. They perform the function of rousing the conscience of society against several kinds of evil prevalent, sometimes even under the guise of law, rule, convention or custom. Such customs come together to keep the individual down, suffocating under the burden of restrictions, finally expedite his total collapse. The writer participates in the struggle against such corruption with all sincerity, moral fidelity and commitment. Identifying and presenting objectionable elements in society with the idea of focussing public attention on them so as to make them think of possible solutions, is in itself an act of social duty and commitment. Obviously, more than the function of a simple photographic camera is expected from the committed writer whose creative faculty sifts and chooses, eliminates and sharpens.

The second approach to literature in the European tradition is Naturalism. It implies that "man's moral beliefs and values require no supernatural sanction, but can be explained in terms of natural causes, including in this case biological and psychological causes. The view also implies that there is no transcendent purpose in the universe, and that man is not free in any unique sense."[22] According to Emile Zola, a practioner of this approach, Naturalism, is expected "to possess a knowledge of the machinery of his intellectual and sensory manifestation, under the influence of heredity and environment, such as physiology shall give them to us and then finally to exhibit man living in social conditions produced by himself which he modifies daily and in the heart of which he himself experiences a continual transformation."[23]

The fact of powerlessness has caused men to view themselves as subjected to the forces of nature. To be without power is to be unable to exert influence upon the universe. This condition is conducive to the flourishing of naturalism, the application of the principles of scientific and socio-economic determinism to literature. Of the two schools of naturalism—*socio-economic determinism,* emphasizing social and economic factors in precipitating man's actions, and *biological determinism,* emphasizing the "given" in man's personality, particularly his hereditary animal nature—the former school is the more optimistic since it places the responsibility for man's action within the control of the society of man. Such ambivalent actions on the part of the society only lead to confusion, and the explosive release of aggressions. In the end, fateful resignation to those forces which cannot be controlled moves men to symbolically accept the validity of the law of the society.

The school of biological determinism is more pessimistic since it defines the locus for control of man's actions within the realm of nature. In the world view of men who are powerless, that which forces subjugation is perceived as antagonistic. Nature, the antagonist, controls the universe; in Nature, power rules. Evil is a matter of course; weakness is man's greatest fear. This view of the machinations of nature is psychologically congruent with the perception of evil as a nemesis which will be eradicated only when nature itself is eradicated.

Repeated stress on the fatalistic attitude towards life is the most conspicuous aspect of naturalism. Naturalistic writers like Zola, Maupassant, and Balzac presented certain inevitability of consequences due to factors of heredity and environment. They introduced characters around whom an invisible network gets tightened, defeating all their attempts to save themselves from tragic fall. Refuting the charge that this approach was fatalistic, Zola draws a clear distinction between 'Fatalism' and 'Determinism'. Determinism differs from fatalism upon which no one can act at all. Fatalism assumes that the appearance of any phenomenon is necessary apart from its conditions, while determinism is just the condition essential for the appearance of any phenomenon, and such appearance is never forced, "the moment that we act, on the determining cause of phenomenon, we cease to be fatalists."[24]

Henrik Ibsen has used the technique of naturalism very effectively proving how the forces of heredity exert a vitiating influence over the fates of individuals, thwarting their attempts to emerge unscathed from agonizing situations in life and plunging them headlong into tragedy. The strength of individual character and determination proves to be ineffective. Social and hereditary factors together form the modern equivalent of Nemesis.

These writers stress the deterministic aspects of modern life where society, instead of classical Nemesis, takes toll of human happiness, by repeatedly defeating their attempts to reform themselves. The inevitability of the nature of ending and the cause-and-effect pattern, give their writings a naturalistic character. Given the details of heredity and social or domestic environment, the individual's character is moulded in a definite form, heading towards the irrevocable end. The audience could anticipate the tragic ending with scientific precision.

Naturalist writers are known not only for a realistic portrayal of life but also for the philosophic determinism and its specific influence, the social environment—and that in an uncommonly narrow sense—almost to the exclusion of all others. Their characters fall under the power of that amorphous and hostile force known as society. Once trapped, they further complicate their lives by committing errors of judgement, and their weakness of character becomes apparent in their tendency to despair. This fact, coupled with their sense of futility, underscores their pessimistic attitude towards society.

Quoting F. H. Heineman, Gerald Rabkin refers to Jean-Paul Sartre as "the philosopher as well as the artist of commitment" and quotes Hazel Barnes's meaning of the French word "Engager", having "both the idea of involvement and the idea of deliberate commitment."[25] The terms engagement and commitment are frequently interchanged. Engagement or commitment arose as an aesthetic problem when the French existentialists attempted to redefine the purpose of art. Since French existentialism is an activist philosophy, Sartre's position is not one of detachment. Man is in the world here and now, must act upon the existentialist fact in order to achieve freedom and self-realisation. Sartre attempts to show the necessity of a committed literature. He affirms that literature must be committed.

> Existentialism is a modern movement encompassing a variety of themes, among them the doctrine that individual existence determines essence, that man has absolute freedom of choice but that there are no rational criteria serving as a basis for choice, and the general claim that the universe is absurd, with an emphasis on the phenomenon of anxiety and alienation ... it is scientific naturalism, human life and conduct are held to be products of mechanical laws or forces, physical or psychological, and man has no real freedom ...[26]

Existentialism, therefore, begins with the fact of individual consciousness as the basis of any philosophical interpretation of life. The study of man, his inner conflicts and genuine choices, his significance in the drama of personal relationships and his responsibility to his fellowmen and to God, these are the elements of human existence.

The emphasis is on the words, 'choice', 'responsibility' and 'commitment'. Man is free to make his choice, and once he does it, he is responsible for the outcome, and is committed to it. It is in this sense of the inexorable and the irrevocable choice, frightening in its finality, that the essence of existentialism is found. 'Existentialism' means something deeper, fuller and richer than 'life'. It signifies not merely physical existence, but also the warmth and complexity of self-consciousness. Hence the use of the term 'existentialism' reinforces the view that philosophy must base its conclusions on life, feeling, passion, and will, and not on intellectual abstractism.

In his book *Existentialism and Humanism*, Sartre explains the essence of his philosophical concepts.

> Man is nothing else but that which he makes of himself. The first principle of existentialism is its 'subjectivity'. Man is, indeed, a project, ... man cannot pass beyond human subjectivity ... our responsibility is thus much greater than we had supposed, for it concerns mankind as a whole ...[27]

Sartre notes that man is considered a product of several factors beyond his control. Existentialism, on the other hand, he explains, is optimistic as a man gets an opportunity—the freedom to choose.

> What is at the very centre of existentialism, is the absolute character of free commitment, by which every man realizes himself i.e., realizing a type of humanity -- a commitment always understandable, to no matter whom i.e., no matter what epoch and its bearing upon the relativity of the cultural pattern which may result from such absolute commitment. [He adds:] Man makes himself: he is not found ready-made; he makes himself by the choice of his

morality and he cannot but choose a morality: such
is the pressure of circumstances upon him.[28]

Since the choice is irrevocable, it becomes a strong commitment or a
binding promise on the part of every man to make positive decisions
which will prove right for himself and for society. Choice in political
and social matters thus becomes a matter of commitment to the cause
of the betterment of society, be it through political or any other
means. It denotes the moral responsibility on the part of the writers.
Presenting the truth, exposing the hypocrisy, and driving home the
imperative necessity of urgent reform at the moral, social, political or
religious levels form the functions of modern art.

Here it is relevant to note that the European point of view of the
commitment of art and the African point of view coincide. Leopold
Senghor (as Ron Karenga quotes), declares that all African art has at
least three characteristics: "it is functional, collective, and committing
or committed."[29] Karenga explains it elaborately. These characteristics are not only traditionally valid but inspiring and make art
revolutionary too. It is functional in the sense that it must be
utilitarian and it dismisses the false doctrine of 'art for art's sake' as
a hoax and myth. All art reflects the value system from which it
springs. For, if the artist created only for himself and not for others,
he would lock himself somewhere and write just for himself. But he
does not do that. On the contrary, he invites others to listen to him
and subjects his work to the scrutiny of his people for their appreciation and evaluation. No art can flourish in vacuum and the evaluation cannot be a favourable one if the work of art is not functional
and utilitarian.

The second characteristic of art in his view is that it must be collective.
It must be from the people and must be returned to the people in a
form more beautiful and colourful than it was in real life. He who
turns a blind eye to his own people will find himself sterile. A writer
is the product of his own milieu and epoch. He is no more than the

context to which he owes his existence. He owes his art to the context and therefore he must be accountable to the people of that context.

Art and people should flourish or decay together. It must move with the masses and be moved by them. The artist must express his appreciation for the people and all they represent and his disdain for everything that threatens their existence. He must move forward with the people with the positive pace rooted in the reality of their situation. He must be with them where they are and take them where they should be.

Whether the emphasis on collective art destroys the individuality of the artist is a relevant question. Individualism is a luxury that the artist cannot afford. Since he owes his existence to his context a writer has no individuality, he has only a personality. Individuality is 'me' in spite of everyone and personality is 'me' in relation to everyone. The one is an insipid isolation and vanity and the other is an important involvement and vitality. The individual is an essence of humanity. The writer is an inseparable part of society and the one complements the other. Individuality implies a false independence; the writer and the society derive value and meaning in a real interdependence. It is an expression of uniqueness of the writer, not in isolation from but in relation to the society in which he lives.

Another relevant question, concerning the artist who rejects the social interpretation of art is whether he should have freedom to do something or freedom from the restrictions that prohibit him from doing something. He demands a socio-political right and that makes art social first and aesthetic second. Art is not an independent living thing, it lives through the people and through the meaning and message people give it. A writer depends upon the language, myth and imagery created by the people. An artist may have freedom to do what he wishes as long as it does not take away from the people the freedom to be protected from those images, words and sounds that are negative to their life and detrimental to their development. It is good to bear in mind the truth of the proverb, "one hand washes the other."

Art must be committing. It must commit the people to revolution and transformation. This is commitment to the struggle; a commitment that includes the artist and the observer. Art will revive, inspire, and give enough courage to face another frustrating day. It must not teach resignation. All art must contribute to revolutionary change and also preserve everything that is good for humanity. If it does not, it is invalid. Art will make people love, and unwillingly though necessarily, to make war too. They will not cry for spilt milk or lost opportunity but find meanings in those things that remain. Art must remind them of their love for each other and their commitment to the revolutionary struggle which must be fought and won.

Chinua Achebe declared in the course of a discussion that an artist is committed to art which is "committed to people".[30] By Aesthetics it is meant those qualities of excellence which a culture discerns from its works of art. Art is made by man for man, and, therefore, according to the needs of man, his qualities of excellence. The artists are not simply receivers of aesthetics; they are creators of aesthetics. They are in a position to create, and society will endorse or reject what they create.

Art has a social purpose and it belongs to the people. Art is social, political, economic, religious and anthropological. The total life of the people is reflected in art. It is all inclusive and all embracing. It does not attempt to exclude anything that is related to the people.

Art cannot be on the side of the oppressor. It is in the service of the people. It is not created to dominate and destroy them. It is created by the people for their own development. The artist tries to use whatever is around and presses it into the service of the people. Art is based on morality. Morality is basic to the nature of art. In a work of art we are confronted with the way we treat each other in society and in politics.

It is against this background of shifting emphasis in the nature and function of literature that the question of black American writers, the inheritors of African and European traditions as committed artists, poses a challenge. The black writer in America "has to locate himself as a Negro with a double commitment: to share in the life of the Americans as a whole, and to assert his cultural importance, so that he is not integrated in the white culture on the white man's terms."[31] How committed these writers have been, to what ideology, and, how far, is at all, their art has been influenced by their commitment will be the points for investigation.

§ § §

NOTES

1.   J. A. Cuddon, *A Dictionary of Literary Terms* (London: André Deutch Ltd., 1977), p. 139.

2.   William Horosz, *The Crisis of Responsibility: Man as the Source of Accountability* (Norman: Univ. of Oklahoma Press, 1975), p. 248.

3.   Gerald Rabkin, *Drama and Commitment* (Bloomington: Indiana University Press, 1964), p. 14.

4.   The followers of Lord Buddha commit themselves to "(1) the founder himself as the 'Awakened One' (2) his exemplary and holy life, his teachings and his experiences (dharma); and (3) the community (Sangha) itself, sustained by the memory of his personality and

24   R. Jothiprakash

teaching." in "Buddhism: Buddhism in India", Mircea Eliade, ed. *The Encyclopedia of Religion*, Vol. 2, (New York: Macmillan Publishing Company, 1987), p. 354.

5.   Gerald Rabkin, op.cit., p. 4.

6.   Thomas Gray, "Elegy Written in a Country Churchyard", 11. P. 55-56.

7.   Gerald Rabkin, op.cit., pp. 6, 7.

8.   George Steiner, "The Writer and Communism", *Language and Silence* (New York: Atheneum, 1958, rpt. 1967), p. 357.

9.   John Mander, *The Writer and Commitment* (West Port, Connecticut: Greenwood Press Publishers, 1961, rpt. 1975), p. 13.

10.   LeRoi Jones, "Afro-American Literature and Class Struggle", *Black American Literature Forum*, 14:1, (1980), p. 8.

11.   George Orwell, *The Collected Essays, Journalism and Letters*, Vol. 2, ed. Sonia Orwell and Ian Angus, (Harmondsworth, Middx: Penguin Books, 1970), p. 152.

12.   James Vinson, ed., *20th Century Drama* (London: The Macmillan Press Ltd., 1983), p. 209.

13.   Raman Selden, *The Theory of Criticism* (London: Longman, 1988), p. 42.

14.   Roger Fowler, *A Dictionary of Modern Critical Terms* (London: Routledge and Kegan Paul, 1973), p. 156.

15.   *The New Columbia Encyclopedia* (New York: Columbia University Press, 1975), p. 2284.

16.   Eric Bentley, *The Playwright as Thinker: A Study of Drama in Modern Times* (New York: Harcourt, Brace and World, 1967) p. 4.

17.   H. Gustav Klans, ed., *The Socialist Novel in Britain: Towards the Recovery of a Tradition* (Brighton: The Harvester Press, 1982), p. 1.

18.   Cited in Ibid., pp. 77 and 115.

19.   Cited in Stern J. P., *On Realism* (London: Routledge and Kegan Paul, 1973), pp. 180-81.

20.   Bernard Shaw, *Complete Plays with Prefaces*, Vol. III, (New York: Dodd, Mead, and Co., 1963), p. 19.

21.   Ramsden Balmforth, *The Problem Play and Its Influence on Modern Life and Thought* (London: Allen and Unwin, 1928), p. 13.

22.   *Caxton's Encyclopedia*, Vol. IV, p. 476.

23.   Cited in Stern's *What was Naturalism* (New York: Appleton Century Crofts, 1959) p. 56.

24.   Ibid., p. 57.

25.   Gerald Rabkin, op.cit., p. 8.

26.   *The New Universal Library*, Vol. II (London: Caxton Publishing Company, 1968), pp. 301-02.

27.   Jean-Paul Sartre, *Existentialism and Humanism*, trans. Philip Mairet (London: Methuen Ltd., 1970), p. 29.

28.   Ibid., p. 47.

29.   Ron Karenga, "Black Cultural Nationalism" in Addison Gayle, Jr., *Black Aesthetic* (New York: Doubleday and Co., 1971), p. 33.

30.   F. L. Standley and L. H. Pratt, *Conversations with James Baldwin* (Jackson: University Press of Mississippi, 1989), p. 216.

31.   Ezekiel Mphahlele, "African Writer and Commitment", in *Voices in the Whirlwind and Other Essays* (New York: Hill and Wang, 1964), p. 195.

CHAPTER TWO

BLACK AMERICAN LITERATURE

As a preliminary step towards the outlining of the genesis and evolution of the literature of the blacks in America, a clarification of the various terms designating the American descendants of African peoples is in order. The word "negro" is derogatory and it is deliberately reductive. The negro has been taught that he is nobody and that blackness is a badge of biological depravity and a sign of worthlessness. As an audacious appreciation of their heritage and their "historical determination to define and name themselves, 'Negro', first capitalized in 1930, is a socio-economic term that was popular from about 1880 to 1960".[1]

During the "Black Power" and "Black Arts Movement" of the 1960's, "the semantics of self-definition made it *de rigueur* amongst the young that the term 'Negro' be supplanted by the term 'Black'".[2] The terms "African American", "Afroamerican", "Afro-American", and "Black American" were also popular in affirming the common legacy of people of the African continent in America and in developing a sense of their own value. These terms are emblematic of an awakened racial pride, a pride fostered by their African roots and by their American heritage.

As a consequence of prejudice against hyphenated ethnic designations, in some quarters the term "Afro-American" is not much preferred.

"Black" as a skin colour conflicts with "black" as a group-name because of the varying colour shades within the group arising out of the miscegenation and mixed blood lines which can neither be denied nor concealed leading to some uncertainties and reluctance in its use.

But these two terms are the more common contemporary designations used synonymously and interchangeably.

The black American writers up to about 1960 called themselves "Negroes", and their productions "Negro Literature". Hence references to these writers, their writings and quotations contain the term "Negro". Otherwise, for general use in the book the term "black American" or simply "black" is employed.

This is also in conformity with Richard Wright's view since he called his autobiography: *Black Boy.*

The blacks were brought to America from Africa in slaveships and in chains during the early decades of the sixteenth century. For the first twenty-five years after their arrival, their status remained that of indentured servants "who had bound themselves to work for masters for a specified length of time in return for paying the cost of their transportation across the Atlantic."[3] But it was not many years before it became common practice to hold a black servant after his term had expired. By 1640 Negro slavery had gained a foothold and the period of service was extended indefinitely taking on the hallmark of slavery. The increased need for the cheap source of labour provided by the blacks paved the way for Negro slavery.

"E Pluribus Unum," the national motto of the United States of America means "one from many." This motto, adopted at the outbreak of the American Revolution, was initially used in a political sense, to signify the fact that out of thirteen separate states one new sovereign power had been established. It has also come to connote that America is made up of many peoples from many lands, having become a nation of nations. The blacks from the continent of Africa were among the very first to arrive in America. "Except for the Indian the Negro is America's oldest ethnic minority.... the Negro's roots in the original thirteen colonies sink deeper than those of any other group from across the Atlantic."[4]

The blacks were, thus, the first who were brought to America as early as 1619 and, from the beginning, they profoundly influenced the changing pattern of American life and culture. The new slaves were systematically cut off from tribal and familial roots by plantation owners. They were sold and resold in defiance of family ties, sexually exploited, forced to take up the name of the white oppressors regardless of actual parentage. They found themselves isolated, not only unable to speak the language of their masters, but often unable to speak to one another as well. This brutal severance of all interpersonal and cultural relationship left them bereft of legitimacy and identity. It had an unwholesome impact on their personality. The deleterious results of this deindividualization made them rootless and nameless. Yet, they managed to survive.

Undoubtedly the black American is the only American who has had to rely so exclusively on the American environment in order to recreate his identity. The Americanness of the black is reflected in his literature.

White Americans have at least had their European institutions, values, and traditions to cling to, or modify, or rebel against. The Negro could only model his culture after the white master's civilization that surrounded him. He could not reach back into time or history to seek his roots.

These blacks and their descendants have been suffering centuries of humiliation and abuse and denial of their civil rights by terror and evasion. They have been the victims of colour prejudice and social deprivation. They continue to fight against rocklike intransigence and sophisticated manipulation of the whites by various methods and their literature forms one of the potent weapons in their crusade and protest against social ills.

The emergence of black writers into the forefront of the literary scene in America is a recent phenomenon. They write for those people for whom a voice has not yet been found, or who attempt in vain to take their destiny in their own hands. They have access to a larger world of social degradation, suffering, poverty and hopelessness. Their private hell, by its very racial nature, raises larger issues of human rights and social responsibilities. When they document their own predicaments and the persecution of their community, their writings reflect their social and cultural context. They, like other writers try to "step out into the universality by first going through the narrow door of the particular."[5]

They have learnt to articulate the most abject kind of misery in artistic terms. Their ability to transcribe the painful facts of their existence without any trace of bitterness or anger speaks of their self-assurance born of strong commitments.

Instead of being nagged by feelings at being black, the black authors try to seek their own destiny in defiance of the ruthless social order and to treat the race neurosis more as the white man's liability than the black man's burden. "And thus for the black writer to explore and to exhibit the rich complexity of Negro life is for him not only to assist his own people toward a deeper understanding of themselves but is for him also to be an agent of self-discovery for the nation at large."[6]

The work of the black American writer symbolizes the response of his creative imagination as an individual reaction to the black's social experience.

Black American literary tradition is multidimensional. It is the literature of the black community and it is the assertion of the whole of humanity. It is an integral part of American literature, but it is also implicitly an attack upon the insolent assumptions of the American society. It has been nurtured and enriched by writers, greatly concerned with ideology. It is the response of the creative imagination of the black as an individual, his reaction to his social experience in America and his fated involvement in the American reality. "Today the essential characteristic of the response is an intense concern with literary discipline and technique, together with a profound social commitment."[7] While transforming themselves, the black writers hope to promote the transformation of society too.

A black writer's conception of himself and the variety of his responses to his condition, enable him to confront American society as an artist as well as a maligned and marginalised human being. This conception encourages him to protest not only against the fallacy and folly of the racial situation but against all the evil forces that all artists and writers must protest against. Social protest is never antithetical to art. However, the urgencies of social protest cannot be invoked as an excuse for shoddy, undisciplined writing. Writing without artistic quality can only lead to inept and ineffective protest literature. Such writing is, in fact, neither protest nor literature. It is only an act of self-indulgence, a long-sustained scream at society and an expression of rage, nothing more.

The literature created by the black Americans is an attempt to explain their peculiar predicament, first to themselves and then to the white society and the rest of the world. Their search for solutions to their problems leads to a protest against the irrational racial situation, to the development of creative imagination and thus, ultimately, to a new concern for art and ideology. Indeed, for the writer, a serious and purposeful commitment to racial justice and social action requires the most intense devotion to literary technique and artistic discipline. There need not be any dichotomy between a purely literary work and a work in the tradition of social protest.

An excellent fusion of commitment to art and ideology is found in the black American writings. One can discern a fundamental nexus between artistic means, that is, technique and discipline, on the one hand and social and moral conviction on the other.

During their prolonged period of slavery, the black Americans were too preoccupied with the demands of survival to find much time for the formal pursuit of literary art. Yet, they did, from the on set of their long struggle for full citizenship, produce an informal literature. The literature produced by them was oral. Knowledge about the past, and about their customs and traditions of the group was transmitted orally in the form of tales, proverbs, songs, and riddles from one generation to another.

One must consider the oral tradition of their cultural expression -- their folklore, the rich body of stories and songs -- that has served as the source of much of their literary inspiration. Nearly all black American folklore is descended from African oral traditions. A separate black American sub-culture formed within the shell of American life which missed the bounties of general education and material progress, and remained a largely oral, self-contained society with its own unwritten history and literature.

Their folklore reveals a great deal about the way they viewed themselves and others, about the ways that they have amused themselves and sustained themselves in an often hostile culture, and about the ways that they have disguised their actual feelings and opinions from white society. The exaggerated tales of humour, legends of famous folk heroes, slave stories, animal tales, blues, spirituals and work songs developed as a result of the oral tradition. The oral tradition gradually gave way to the written tradition in the history of American slavery. A relatively privileged class of "house niggers" developed. This class, often represented by the racially mixed relatives of the old master, soon constituted a small, elite caste within slavery, whose opportunities for literacy far outstripped those of "field niggers". These "house niggers" began producing written literature which was a remarkable achievement in itself.

"The first known piece of literature written by a black American is a short doggerel titled "Bars Fight", which was written in 1746 by a sixteen-year-old servant-girl named Lucy Terry (1730-1821)."[8] Jupiter Hammon (1718-1806), in 1760, composed a poem entitled "An Evening Thought: Salvation by Christ with Penitential Cries", which was the first known work to be published in America by a black. Throughout this initial period black authors depended upon a white audience. So their work often reflected the stereotypes born of white presumption.

The black writers of the eighteenth century, most of whom were living in New England, where they did not experience the miseries of southern plantation etc. wrote relatively little on the subject of race and virtually nothing which corresponded in subject or intensity to the black protest writing of the nineteenth century. They were committed to religious themes and overlooked the obvious evils of enforced human servitude and viewed the peculiar institution as the glorious means by which the otherwise heathen Africans were brought into the Christian fold.

Phillis Wheatley (1754-1784), the African-born servant of John Wheatley, was given educational opportunities because of her obvious intelligence and thereby became well-versed in the Bible and in the English classics. Her *Poems on Various Subjects, Religious and Moral*, was published in London in 1773.

In spirituality the slaves achieved an art form that provided balm for their weary souls. In her poem, "On Being Brought from Africa to America", Miss Wheatley apologizes for her heritage and pleads that even blacks "may be refined" through Christianity:-

> 'Twas mercy brought me from my Pagan land,
> Taught my benighted soul to understand
> That there's a God, that there's a Saviour too:
> Once I redemption neither sought nor knew.
> Some view our sable race with scornful eye;
> "Their colour is a diabolic dye"

Remember Christians, Negroes, black as Cain,
May be refined, and join the angelic train"[9]

Sterling Brown says of Miss Wheatley that, "the real griefs she experienced herself or could have witnessed are missing" and that this is "cause for regret".[10]

While religion provided an avenue of escape from the realities of life, literature was clearly perceived as an important weapon by the slaves who succeeded in articulating their plight and in exhibiting an imaginative capacity to use this weapon as a potent instrument for liberation. The slave narratives such as (a) Briton Hammon's *A Narrative of the Uncommon Sufferings and Surprising Deliverance of Briton, A Negro Man* (1760) (b) *A Narrative of the Lord's Wonderful Dealings with J. Marrant, a Black* (1785) and (c) *The Interesting Narrative of the Life of Olandah Equiane, or Gustavus Vassa, the African;* (1789) became best-selling favorites among American and English abolitionists, since they were assaults upon the institution of slavery and were directed at the conscience of America. For example, James M. Whitefield (1823-1878) in the title poem of his only published volume *America and Other Poems* (1853) expresses his anger:

America, it is to thee,
Thou boasted land of liberty,
It is to thee I raise my song,
thou land of blood, and crime, and wrong.[11]

The slave narratives which employed episodic structure, mingled picturesque details with passages of moral persuasion and used the first person point of view, served a more militant purpose by dispelling the myths of the pro-slavery argument, urging the other slaves to secure their freedom by flight or by open rebellion and at the same time exhorted the white readers to take action against slavery in

America by recounting incidents that horrified or repelled the readers.

In 1827, the first black newspaper *Freedom's Journal* began publication in New York City, and in 1831 the most famous of the abolitionist newspaper, William Lloyd Garrison's *The Liberator*, was founded in Boston.

George Moses Horton (1797-1883), whose collection of poems *Hope of Liberty* (1829), is considered to be one of the first works devoted largely to themes of protest, openly posed the seminal question of slavery in what claimed to be a democratic society.

Slave memoirs were the dominant literary form published by black American during the nineteenth century prior to the Civil War. They are extensions of the folk-tale tradition in that they reveal and repeat common cultural experiences -- recount similar tales of the horrors of slavery, cruel overseers, separation of black families, and sexual abuse heaped upon black women by their white masters.

Frederick Douglass (1817-1895), William Wells Brown and David Walker among others, emerged as effective spokesmen for their cause. Douglass's autobiography was originally published as a slave *Narrative of the Life of Frederick Douglass (1845)* was republished as *My Bondage and My Freedom* in 1855, with certain further details. It was further expanded as *Life and Times of Frederick Douglass* in 1891, and was elaborated one last time in 1892, under the same title. Through his writings he championed emancipation, fought disenfranchisement, worked for equality in education and employment and endorsed decent treatment of the working class generally:

"I assert then that poverty, ignorance and degradation are the combined evils, or in other words, these constitute the social disease of the free coloured people of the United States. To deliver them from this triple malady, is to improve and elevate them, by which I mean, simply to put them on an equal footing with their white fellow countrymen in the sacred right to 'Life, Liberty and the pursuit of happiness'."[12] He advocated the use of direct political action as the most effective means of overthrowing slavery.

William Wells Brown (1816-1884) was America's first black novelist and he was single-minded in his commitment to abolish slavery. His *My Three Years in Europe*, (1852) was the first travel book by a black American. In 1858 he wrote *The Escape*, or a *Leap for Freedom*, which was the first play by a black American. He was also the first major black American to exploit the tragic mulatto theme. His autobiography, *The Narrative of William Wells Brown (1847)* describes his successful escape from his white master in 1834, and his subsequent development as an orator, novelist and playwright. *Clotel or The President's Daughter* (1852) recounts the story of the two mulatto girls Clotel and Althesa, the daughters of Thomas Jefferson, the writer of the Declaration of American Independence, and one of the presidents of the great republic. Brown was a man committed to the ideal of social justice and his purpose was to shake into wakefulness the American conscience to the evils of slavery.

Little time was wasted on subjects other than slavery and the white problems during the earliest periods, though by 1861, Frances Ellen Watkins Harper (1825-1911) argued that black authors should concern themselves with feelings that are general rather than black themes. Harper, who wrote America's first published short story by a black author ("The Two Offers" in the *Anglo-African Magazine* for September-October 1859), attempted in both her poetry and prose, to include experiences transcending racial limitations. In fact, she was one of the first American women to attack openly the "double standard" in sexual morality. She proclaimed in her poem "A Double Standard" that what is wrong in women's life cannot be right in man's. Another writer, Martin Delaney (1812-1885), broke with melodramatic stereotypes by showing characters capable of good or evil, no matter what their race. He urged the colonization in Central America and Africa, by the blacks.

In 1852, the most influential novel, *Uncle Tom's Cabin*[13] by Harriet Beecher Stowe, was published. Mrs. Stowe, a white American, a product of the intellectual aristocracy of New England is an example of the white American's interest in the abolition of slavery. Her emphasis was clearly on the evils of slavery, the fragmentation of black families by sale and the brutality inseparable from the pursuit and recapture of fugitive blacks. The significance of the novel was more in its social effects than in its artistic qualities.

Uncle Tom's Cabin "has been considered a strange hybrid of polemic and sentimental melodrama, a work that helped instigate the Civil War".[14] It is also thought to be perpetuating "the misconceptions, ... the wrong headedness, the distortions and wishful thinkings" about black Americans which have made her hero Tom connote "Meek servility and offensive minstrel-like traits" that many of them "would rather be called 'nigger' than 'Uncle Tom'".[15]

By giving flesh and blood reality to the inhuman system, *Uncle Tom's Cabin* proved to be a touchstone for antislavery sentiment. Stowe was hardly the first to call attention to slavery's destruction of both black and white families but her novel perfectly combined the tradition of the sentimental novel and rhetoric of antislavery polemic. In scene after scene the fragmentation of black households and the corrosive moral effect on white conscience is her focal point.

Stowe "speaks with the prophets of old, reminding the nation of its historical commitments, recording its present struggle, warning of the impending wrath of the Almighty, if the nation should betray its covenant and its destiny."[16] The claim that *Uncle Tom's Cabin* in any way caused the Civil War and that "Mrs. Stowe has invented the Negro novel"[17] and "for better or worse, it was Mrs. Stowe who invented American blacks for the imagination of the whole world"[18] must be considered in relation to her popularity based on her commitments to Christian faith.

In spite of the intensity of her feelings while writing, Mrs. Stowe showed admirable tact in refraining from attacks on the people of the south. Her second novel *Dred*(1856) modelled its hero on Nat Turner who was a black peasant and preacher. He dared against slavery in Virginia in 1831. With five followers Turner slaughtered sixty whites and later over hundred slaves were killed in retaliation. After this abortive rebellion southern attitudes towards slaves became increasingly reactionary and intransigent. Never again would the south feel safe with slaves. Stowe depicted Turner as a fanatical religious prophet misguided by visions and also as a freak and his rebellion as a deviation from the expected docility of the blacks.

She was successful in depicting Uncle Tom as a pious, passive and non-violent gentleman committed to self-sacrifice. When she wrote about a black as a rebel she chose Turner, the rebel who failed because of his unchristian disposition.

In 1863, Abraham Lincoln signed the Emancipation Proclamation and, by the last decade of the nineteenth century, the social and literary climate for black Americans in the north had changed gradually and enough education and stability had grown within the middle class to stimulate literary expression. This period was the first to produce writers who, in spite of persisting oppressive racial conditions, were able to maintain in their writing significant artistic detachment from those conditions. Race relations, especially in the south, were at an all-time low. During Reconstruction the southern white reaction against blacks who were asserting their new rights began. The Ku Klux Klan began to flourish with its regular night-riding sprees of terror, mutilation and arson. In addition, the Ku Klux Klan and other racial organizations expanded their activities as a supplement to the "Jim Crow" laws which still denied blacks the right to vote and the right to receive decent education. In 1883, the

U.S. Supreme Court ruled that the Civil Rights Act of 1875 was unconstitutional and in 1896, the same court declared that "separate but equal" public accommodations were "reasonable" provisions for blacks.

In spite of these dismal and disastrous social conditions a number of writers, committed to the perfection of literary art forms, emerged during this period.

Paul Laurence Dunbar (1872-1906) was a gifted poet whose blackness forced him into the production of verse in dialect and it was his dialect poetry which made him the best known black poet since Phillis Wheatley. It is of course significant that three out of his four novels are not about blacks at all, and he depicted himself as a white youth in his autobiography, *The Uncalled* (1898). He seldom dealt with themes of protest and he rarely mentioned racial injustice. His novel *The Sport of the Gods* (1902) and his short story, "The Lynching of Jube Benson" are exceptions. He unwittingly reinforced the notion of many whites that social and economic opportunities were available to all who were industrious and frugal and "wait", thus indirectly supporting the "accommodationist" policy of Booker T. Washington (1858-1915), who was a pragmatic and conservative leader. He was the founder of the Tuskegee Institute in Alabama.

He preached a message of compromise, of humility, and of patience. His works supported the stereotype of the black as a satisfied peasant, docile servitor, a creature who had a place, knew it and would keep it in order to lead a decent life.

He argued that it was vain for the blacks to attempt to make the leap to equality at once; advocated the gospels of hard work, self-help and thrift. The blacks must prove themselves, must show tangibly that they deserved the blessing of Emancipation. His accommodationist policy suited the then prevalent conditions and prejudices. The foundations of race advancement must be economic not political, moral not confrontational. His emphasis on the practical and possible made the blacks meek not militant, industrious not indolent, conforming not complaining. In short, he wanted the black American to lift himself by his own bootstrap. His advice did not take into account the fact that the black was barefoot. His policies were interpreted as self-perpetuating and as permanent acceptance of servility and hence he was called a tyrant and traitor to the cause of black dignity.

The short stories of Charles Waddell Chesnutt (1858-1932) demonstrated that black characters could be created without recourse to traditional stereotypes endorsed by B. T. Washington.   When Chesnutt's stories began appearing in the *Atlantic Monthly* in 1887, it was not generally known that their author was a black and his racial identity was kept as a secret for almost a decade.

Chesnutt displays an excellent grasp of dialect. The insights of his characters lift the stories to a plane on which universal observations are made.   He was successful in creating "artist's reality" which enabled him to transcend the racial conditions. His novels *The House Behind the Cedars (1900) The Marrow of Tradition (1901)* and *The Colonel's Dream(1905)* are his major contributions.

James Weldon Johnson (1871-1938) presents the protagonist of his novel *The Autobiography of an Ex-Coloured Man* (1912) as a man who finds himself torn between his commitment to the black race and his desire for success for himself and for his family. It also deals openly with the game of "passing" practised by Chesnutt.   The protagonist appears white because of his new England upbringing and even though he has hopes of a brilliant future in music as a "white", he is nonetheless committed to live "black"; but after much psychological torture "passes" permanently into white society, marries a white, and becomes a successful businessman but at a considerable moral cost. Johnson composed "Lift Every Voice and Sing" which had the approval of Booker T. Washington and became the "Negro National Anthem." He published three volumes of verse and an excellent study of black culture in New York, *Black Manhattan* (1930) as well as his autobiography, *Along This Way*, (1933) written largely to prove that the novel was not, in fact, his autobiography.

William Edward Burghardt DuBois (1868-1963) was the first black to obtain a Ph.D. from Harvard University and became America's most accomplished scholar on race relations, and interpreter of black culture. He established one of the first black studies programs at Atlanta University and founded the periodical *Phylon*. He vociferously attacked Booker T. Washington's accommodationist racial policies. His book *The Souls of Black Folk* (1903) provided an alternative to Washington's approach to racial uplift. In 1905 he formed the Niagara Movement for the improvement of the status of black intellectuals. In 1909 he founded the NAACP (National Association for the Advancement of Colored People), and became the editor of the Association's publication *Crisis*, which provided a forum for the ideas that ran counter to the notions of black inferiority. He was convinced that racial injustice could be dealt with only through international socialist politics and not through patronizing national civil rights organizations. He joined the Communist Party in 1957 and shortly thereafter renounced his American citizenship and in 1910 he moved to Ghana and died there in 1963. His publications include *The Quest of the Silver Fleece* (1911), and *Dark Princess* (1928), *The Souls of Black Folk* and his *Autobiography of W.E.B. DuBois* (1968).

His commitment was to analyse the cultural impact of recently acquired freedom, to foster correct black leadership and to do away with the effects of being forced to lead a culturally dual existence. He says:

> It is a peculiar sensation, this double consciousness,
> this sense of always looking at one's self through the
> eyes of others, of measuring one's soul by the tape of
> a world that looks on in amused contempt and pity.
> One ever feels his two-ness - an American a Negro,

> two souls, two thoughts, two unreconciled striving,
> two warring ideals in one dark body, whose dogged
> strength alone keeps it from being torn asunder.[19]

DuBois appealed to a black audience extolling racial consciousness and pride. It was he who fired the imagination of black intellectuals and paved the way for the emergence of the "New Negro" movement in the 1920's. The resolution of the problem of black "twoness" became the most dominant concern of the "Harlem Renaissance".

As the 20th century dawned, the migration of blacks from the rural south to the urban north began and prejudice toward blacks again intensified. Yet the seeds of literary excellence had been sown. The brilliance of DuBois dominated the black intelligentsia of skilled writers such as James Weldon Johnson, Claude McKay, William Standley Braithwaite and Fenton Johnson, whose literary contributions marked the 'Third Force' in American literature besides the European and African forces.

Alain LeRoy Locke (1886-1954) published *The New Negro* an anthology of black essays, fiction, poetry and drama in which he asserted that black writers "stopped speaking for the Negro" because now "they speak as Negroes. Where formerly they spoke to others and tried to interpret, they now speak to their own and try to express".[20]

The Harlem Renaissance was born out of a celebration of sensuality, a faith in a self liberated from social commitments and a belief in the virtues of improvisation in personal affairs. Jazz was the symbol of the age because of its spontaneity. The black writing tended to emphasize a free self without responsibility to society.

The "plantation" stereotypes and the melodramatic protest of the nineteenth century yielded place to a pride in black artistry, craftsmanship, music and dance and in blackness itself.

The sudden flowering in literature gave voice to the new spirit awakening in blacks which became a part of the general revolt by the writers of the decade against the outmoded moral values of America's industrial society. Black writers found new strength in their own folk culture.

As used in the 20's the term "New Negro" referred to the writers then active in the Negro Renaissance; and also to the black masses, especially the young. The new spirit that pervaded during the 20's was basically a renewal of "self-respect and self-dependence."

The new confidence which characterized the black in the 20's was the outgrowth of many forces.   Militant new leaders arose.   They demanded full civil liberties and an end to segregation. They inspired a great self-assertiveness in their people.   World War I and the resulting mass migration of blacks to the north further disrupted old patterns of life and created new hopes and new problems. The fight for democracy abroad led to greater expectations at home.   The remarkable popularity of Marcus Garvey, (1887-1940) and his Black Nationalism indicated the black masses that their frustrated ambitions could no longer be contained.

The "New Negro" was only apparently phoenix-like, rejuvenating from the ashes of his own degradation. In the 1920's the blacks cracked through the prejudices. The Garvey Movement, fast getting out of bounds, swept the country like a wildfire. J. W. Johnson published an anthology of black verse. The monumental historical studies of the blacks were begun by Carter Woodson and a number of books dealing with black life and aspirations had been published, read, discussed, praised or damned by 1920. The best of Johnson, Cullen, Hughes, McKay and DuBois considerably furthered the interest of white writers and critics in black life and black art expression. They gave validity to the concept of the black as material for serious artistic treatment. Writing by blacks beginning with this period up to the early 30's had two aspects:-

They were extremely arty, self-conscious and experimental. Jean Toomer and Langston Hughes represent it most notably. They enjoyed the winds of literary freedom and even of licence. If their self-conscious experimentation proved nothing lasting, it, at least, worked no harm. But the second aspect was full of contradictions. It showed itself innocent and worldly-wise, wrathful and pleased, preposterous and sober, liberated and bound.

Harlem was largely synthetic of both trends. Jazz music became no longer the uninhibited expression of unlettered muses but a highly refined pattern of musical sounds. Blues became the "torch song".

The writers who gathered in Harlem, the body of whose work is known as the Harlem Renaissance, produced a flood of poems, short stories, novels, and plays highlighting the low life of the Black American masses which were relished by a sizable white reading public which championed black cause. Unfortunately, much of the literature of this period was second-rate stuff satisfying the merriment-seeking Jazz Age readers who desired to taste vicariously a life as different from their own as they could find. With the onslaught of the Depression, the vogue of the black died almost as swiftly as it had emerged.

In rebelling against the social and cultural restraints of their predecessors, the Renaissance writers took an opposite direction that produced an equivalent distortion. Taking their literary cues from the preoccupations of the Jazz Age, they emphasized the black's showmanship, his songs, his dances, and his social pleasures, to the exclusion of other salient ingredients of his life. But they were committed to strengthening each other by real or symbolic acts. They attempted to redefine their past by discovering a more glorious history as it was fancied to have been in Africa.

"The 'Edenic nostalgia' of the black American literature is the black's response to Africa".[21] The image of Africa repeatedly appeared in black poetry. Garvey's Universal Nergo Improvement Association, originally founded in Jamaica in 1914, spread in America in the early 1920's and was in some respects the political embodiment of the black American's concern with Africa as image and fact. Garvey advocated a back-to-Africa policy which assumed that Africa was the spiritual, if not actual, home of the blacks. It was the first dynamically organized mass movement which resulted in the blossoming of black nationalism. Despite its abrupt end--Garvey's projects misfired one after the other and he himself was arrested for fraud and banished--its significance was considerable. For the first time, there was pride and fulfillment in the minds of the black masses who had previously been ashamed of their colour.

The nationalist aspects of the Renaissance literature of the twenties--the fierce race pride, the constant sense of ethnic identity, and the lure of Africa--remained a strong factor in the writings of later black authors.

They were committed to the Nationalist tradition and 'proletarian literature' school. Among the writers of the 1930's and 1940's some were influenced by existentialism and the French African literary tradition. They were enthusiastic about the concepts of 'Black Power' and 'Black is Beautiful' and shattered the stereotype of a black character as one grinning, passive and happily acquiescent to his exploitation.

It was in the poetry of James Weldon Johnson, Claude McKay, Langston Hughes and Countee Cullen that black Americans first encountered a large expression in lyric form of their ancestral memories and of their irrefutably fated involvement in the American Dream. The fictional works of George S. Schuyler *Black No More* (1931), Nella Larson *Quick Sand* (1928) and Zora Neale Hurston *Their Eyes were Watching God* (1937) reflected the multifaceted mirror of their existence and a literature of their own emerged.

This period was the first to produce writers who, in spite of oppressive racial conditions, committed themselves to maintain in their writing significant artistic detachment from those conditions. Harlem became the capital of black American cultural life during this period and served as the training ground for most of the major writers who began their career during the twenties.

A number of white writers also treated black themes and contributed to the new interest in black life styles and culture: the drama of Eugene O'Neill *The Emperor Jones*, (1920) and *All God's Chillun Got Wings*, (1923) as well as the fiction of Sherwood Anderson *Dark Laughter*, (1925), DuBose Heyward *Mamba's Daughters*, (1929) and Carl Van Vechten's *Nigger Heaven*, (1926). *The Confessions of Nat Turner* by William Styron is also an attempt, after Mrs. Stowe, by a white author to document the psychological rationale of an incident in the history of blacks through the eyes of the black protagonist.

The first important writer of the Renaissance was Claude McKay (1889-1948), who was born in Jamaica. He came to the U.S.A. in 1912 to study agriculture at the Tuskegee Institute. *Home to Harlem, Banjo* and *Banana Bottom* (1933) were the three novels and *Gingertown* is a book of short stories written by McKay. But it is in his poetry that he will be longest remembered. In his poetry, he expressed the black's determination to protect his human dignity, his cultural worth, and his right to a decent life.

Braithwaite recognised Claude McKay as the first voice in the Harlem Renaissance. His poem "If We Must Die"[22] stirred the blood of all blacks:-

> If we must die, let it not be like hogs
> Hunted and penned in an inglorious spot,
> While round us bark the mad and hungry dogs,
> making their mock at our accursed lot.
> If we must die, oh, let us nobly die,

So that our precious blood may not be shed
In vain; then even the monsters we defy
shall be constrained to honor us though dead;
Oh, Kinsmen! we must meet the common foe!
Though far outnumbered, let us show us brave,
And for their thousand blows deal one death-blow!
What though before us lies the open grave?
Like men we'll face the murderous, cowardly pack,
Pressed to the wall, dying, but fighting back.

Sir Winston Churchill quoted these lines as climax and conclusion of his oration before the joint-houses of the American Congress when he was seeking to draw America into the common effort in World War II. McKay had written it as a defiant answer to lynching and mob violence in the southern states. Churchill made it the voice of the embattled allies as he read aloud "If We Must Die".

The second important writer of the Renaissance, Jean Toomer (1894-1967) published his *Cane* in 1923. With an artist's passion and sympathy for life, he wrote about the black without the surrender or compromise of the artist's vision. So objective was it that we feel that it is a mere accident that birth or association has thrown him into contact with the life he has written about. He would write just as well, about the others, had experience brought him in touch with their existence. *Cane* is a highly successful collection of prose sketches and poems strung together thematically into contrasting pictures of southern peasant life and northern black urban life. It is also about the search for roots and about the penalties a people suffer by being uprooted. *Roots* (1976), the generational opus written by Alex Haley, is his family's origins from Africa through slavery and into the present century. Haley traces his roots and lineage in order to repossess his own history and reveals how the blacks prize their ancestral memories and find themselves as inseparable component of the American culture.

Undoubtedly the most popular writer to emerge from the Renaissance was the poet Langston Hughes (1902-1967), who was born in Missouri. His article, "The Negro Artist and the Racial Mountain" which was widely acclaimed as the literary manifesto of the "New Negro", urged the black artist to make full use of the colourful, distinctive material at his disposal and to interpret the beauty of his own people. He proclaimed:

> We younger Negro artists who create now intend to express our individual dark-skinned selves without fear or shame. If white people are pleased we are glad. If they are not, it doesn't matter .... If colored people are pleased, we are glad. If they are not their displeasure doesn't matter either. We build our temples for tomorrow, strong as we know how, and we stand on top of the mountain free within our-selves.[23]

Hughes popularised an imaginary character Jesse B. Simple, the black Everyman. Simple's conversations with his friend Boyd served as springboard for Hughes's opinions and flights of imagination. Simple, an anti-authoritarian-optimist pokes fun at his own foibles and mocks at the hypocrisy and the shams of his compatriots both black and white and makes his readers feel angry and abashed simultaneously. He is sane and resilient. He is the embodiment of the black's desire to survive and prevail in the face of insuperable odds.

Huges was rightfully called the Dean of black American letters. He reflected the deep black pride in the black heritage. He published poetry *The Weary Blues* (1926) and *Fine Clothes to the Jew* (1927), novels *Not Without Laughter* (1930) *Tambourines to Glory* (1958) and five volumes of "Simple" sketches, a play, two autobiographies *The Big Sea* (1940) and *I Wonder as I Wander* (1956), the history of the NAACP, *Fight for Freedom* (1962) and collections of African writing, black American Folklore, black poetry, black short stories and black humour. He was influenced by the social realism and by the rhythms of jazz.

None of the representatives of the Black Renaissance movement except Hughes succeeded in making any lasting impact on the scene. The running pace of black writing slowed during the thirties.

The second Black Renaissance "did, indeed, have its roots in the work of Richard Wright, who, in a sense, contained within himself the conflicting passions which, for the next four decades, defined the nature of the black American's debate with himself and with his culture".[24]

Richard Wright (1908-1960) through his books *Uncle Tom's Children* (1938), *Native Son* (1940), *Black Boy* (1945), *The Outsider* (1953) and *The Long Dream* (1958) made the voice of the black Americans heard as a truly and universal song which stirred the hearts of men living an existence characterized by marginality and irrational persecution.

With the 1940 publication of *Native Son*, Wright became the first black American author of a best--seller. *Native Son* is the story of a black underclass youth who resorts to violence as a retaliation to the oppression, hatred and incomprehension of the white world. His novels and his moving autobiography *Black Boy* reveal the fact that he, more powerfully than any of his predecessors, realized and recognized the rage lodged in the hearts of the blacks, who had nothing to lose and nothing left to live for and those who have had to endure the bitter social realities that were the consequences of racism.

In his "Blueprint for Negro Writing" Wright set the responsibility upon the black writer, "to furnish moral sanctions for action, to give meaning to blighted lives and to supply motives for mass movements of millions of people.... He is being called upon to do no less than create values by which his race is to struggle, live and die,".[25]

Wright vehemently opposed the writers who pandered to a white audience rather than directing themselves to the needs of black people. In so doing, Wright thought that these writers ignored the black folklore and disowned their responsibility in favour of literary posturing, which however clever and ornamental, were culturally sterile and aesthetically barren.

Richard Wright drew inspiration from black folklore. In his writings he mixed judiciously the personal, the documentary, the factual and the fictional elements.

Wright attempted to administer a rude shock to the American culture out of its lackadaisical conscience and to generate in the black masses a new power of self-affirmation and a fresh resoluteness of purpose in its quest for justice. He conceived of good and evil in terms of man-made creations. Since man has made them man alone can change them.

"The Black Artist's role in America is to aid in the destruction of America as he knows it. His role is to report and reflect so precisely the nature of the society and of himself in that society."[26] Wright realized this responsibility.

Richard Wright in his graphic description of his early life in *Black Boy* has woven the fabric of his evolution as a writer with his social commitments as its warp and artistic commitments as its woof. Life and art are inseparable in Wright's works and he was not an artist who remained impervious to the environment around him. Keneth Kinnamon is of the opinion that "Wright represented the culmination of the tradition of vigorous racial and social protest espoused by writers such as Frederick Douglass and Claude McKay and by much black folklore."[27]

His example proved to be an inspiration and a model to a number of black American writers. In fact no black American writer is immune from Wright's influence. "His work became an effective north star of Negro writing, which helped his successors to find their own directions."[28]

Native Son presents a new approach to the treatment of urban black living. It shows how these dismal conditions twist the social and spiritual development of the blacks. Crime is the inevitable product of a warped society. Wright makes it abundantly clear that individuals such as Bigger Thomas live by a strange and perverted code. They are not likely to succeed by following acceptable standard, so they seek release from the frustration and anger engendered by the shams and hoaxes practiced against them by the white America. And that release comes through the tendency to destroy others and, at the end, themselves.

Wright was committed to prove that a man must have enough control over his environment to feel that he can change it so that it can offer him chances of realizing his innate potentialities; in the absence of such a control, he deems himself to be an alien and undermines the mores and legal codes of his society. He also attempted to reveal the social and psychological effects on human beings who find themselves trapped in these absurd and oppressive conditions and how they unsuccessfully make an existence in such a situation.

Wright joined the Communist Party in 1934. Communism was thought to be a gospel of liberation among the coloured people. According to him the party taught him, "if you possess enough courage to speak out what you are, you will find that you are not alone".[29] For Wright, Marxism became a way of life ordering his experiences provided him with a means of interpreting the urban scene which the Harlem School lacked, provided him with an intellectual framework for understanding his life as a black. A stubborn and uncompromising individualism kept him in constant conflict with the party bureaucracy, leading eventually to his break from the party.

In speaking of the writers who followed Wright, Robert Bone proposes that they may be thought of as forming "the Wright School"[30] of that period.

The writers usually included in this School are Chester Himes, *If He Hollers Let Him Go* (1945) Ann Petry *The Street* (1946), Willard Motley, *Knock on Any Door* (1947). James Baldwin and Ralph Ellison who came strongly under the influence of Wright later broke away from that influence as they wished to move substantially beyond Wright. They protested against an oppressive and coercive racist environment, but to label them as "protest writers" is to cast a pejorative light on them and to limit, unfairly, their commitments. "Wright was praised and damned posthumously because of his apparent commitment to the use of literature as a political weapon in the war against white racism."[31]

The two prominent authors James Baldwin and Ralph Ellison, who had received encouragement from Wright, later found fault with him. The questions how far their commitments towards life and art are different from those of their mentor and why need to be answered.

An attempt to seek answers to these queries leads one to an in-depth study of the writings of Baldwin and Ellison and their commitments.

§ § §

NOTES

1.   Martin Coyle et. al., *Encyclopedia of Literature and Criticism* (London: Routledge, 1991), p. 1137.

2.   Nathan A. Scott, Jr., "Black Literature", in *Harvard Guide to Contemporary American Writing*, ed. Daniel Hoffman, (Cambridge, Mass.: Harvard University Press, 1979), p. 305.

3.   Benjamin Quarles, *The Negro in the Making of America* (New York: The Macmillan Company, 1969), p. 34.

4.   Ibid., p. 7.

5.   Cleanth Brooks, "Irony as a Principle of Structure", in *Literary Opinion in America*, ed. Morton Dauwenzabel (New York: Harper and Bros., 1951), p. 729.

6.   Nathan A. Scott, Jr., op. cit., pp. 340-41.

7.   Herbert Hill, "Introduction", *Anger and Beyond: The Negro Writer in the United States* (New York: Harper and Row Publishers, 1966), p. xiii.

8.   Roger Whitlow, *Black American Literature: A Critical History* (New Jersey: Little-field, Adams & Co., 1974), p. 15.

9.   Ibid., p. 22.

10.   *Negro Poetry and Drama and the Negro in American Fiction* (New York: Atheneum, 1969), p. 6.

11.   Benjamin Brawley, ed. *Early Negro American Writers* (New York: Dover, 1970), p. 228.

12.   "A letter to Mrs. Stowe", from *Black American Literature Essays* ed. David Turner (Columbus, Ohio: Charles E. Merrill Publications Co., 1969), p. 18.

13.   When it appeared in book form in 1852, 50,000 copies were sold within eight weeks, 300,000 within a year, and 1 million in America and England combined by early 1853, according to Eric J. Sundquist, *New Essays on 'Uncle Tom's Cabin'* (New York: Cambridge University Press, 1986), p. 18.

14.   Eric J. Sundquist, "Introduction", Ibid. p. 1.

15.   U. C. Furnas, *Goodbye to Uncle Tom* (New York: William Sloane, 1956), pp. 8-10.

16.   Alice C. Crozier, *The Novels of Harriet Beecher Stowe* (New York: Oxford University Press, 1969), p. 6.

17.   George Eliot, review of *Dred: A Tale of the Great Dismal Swamp* by Harriet Beecher Stowe in *Critical Essays on Harriet Beecher Stowe* ed. Elizabeth Ammons (Boston: G. K. Hall, 1980), p. 43.

18.   Leslie Fiedler, *The Inadvertant Epic: From 'Uncle Tom's Cabin' to 'Roots'* (New York: Simon and Schuster, 1979), p. 26.

19.   *The Souls of the Black Folk* (Chicago,: A. C. McClurg and Company 1903), p. 3.

20.   *The New Negro* (New York: Atheneum, 1968), p. 48.

21.   Irving Howe, *The Decline of the Novel* (London: Gollanz, 1971), p. 95.

22.   Quoted in Herbert Hill, op.cit., p. 13.

23.   *The Nation*, Vol. 122, No. 3181 (1926), p. 694.

24.   C. W. E. Bigsby, *The Second Black Renaissance: Essays in Black Literature* (West Port, Conn.: Greenwood Press, 1980), p. 3.

25.   *New Challenge*, II (Fall 1957), pp. 53-65.

26.   LeRoi Jones, *Home: Social Essays* (New York: William Morrow, 1961), p. 251.

27.   *The Emergence of Richard Wright* (Chicago: University of Illinois Press, 1972), p. 160.

28.   Morris Dickstein, "Wright, Baldwin, Cleaver", *New Letters*, XXXVIII (Winter 1971), pp. 117-124.

29.   "I Tried to be a Communist", *Atlantic Monthly*, 174 (August 1944), p. 62.

30.   *The Negro Novel in America* (New Haven: Yale University Press, 1965), pp. 157-160.

31.   J. H. Bryant, "Wright, Ellison, Baldwin - Exorcising the Demon", *Phylon*, (Vol. XXXVII, No. 2, (1976), p. 174.

CHAPTER THREE

JAMES BALDWIN - PART ONE

James Arthur Baldwin, risen out of the racial nightmare of Harlem to carve a permanent niche for himself in American letters is easily the most gifted and the most disturbing artist of distinction to have appeared in the history of black American literature. "I would place him very high among writers," said Benjamin DeMott, "in part because his work showed a powerful commitment to the right values and had a profound impact for good on our culture."[1]

He was a writer of daring and dignity and his soul witnessed a tug-of-war between two uncompromising urges — one yearning for his African roots and the other lamenting over and rejoicing in its American heritage of insult and injury, of freedom and possibility.

Self-exile was the way shown by his mentor Richard Wright to flee from the fear and rage of American realities. Baldwin sought a home away from home in Paris. But he could neither wean himself completely from the happenings in his native land nor accomplish an enduring truce between his warring urges. He remained a trans-Atlantic commuter for four decades. In this predicament lay the complexity of his fate and the commitments of his life and writings.

Baldwin is well-known for his unique literary style characterized by poetic profusion and power. He is also remembered as an ardent civil rights crusader, a polished pamphleteer, a racial rhetorician, a witness who committed himself to the sacred task of giving testimony to what he had seen, and a prophet praying to God to be merciful and praying for humanity to transform itself, before God metes out His final justice. "Baldwin speaks boldly as a Negro - that is to say, as a human being while recognizing his responsibility to the craft he practices."[2]

He employed more than one prose type and several of the communication media, the newspaper, the theatre and the printed book in order to keep his voice heard and to amuse, stun, exhilarate and exasperate the readers. He was an accusing finger thrust in the face of white America. His function as a writer was irksome and so were his commitments. After all, to write, if taken seriously, is to be subversive and to disturb the peace. The writer does not merely record what happens; he probes. Although Baldwin had earned a reputation for being a harsh critic, and for exposing the grit and grime in American race relations, he was actually most committed to the problems and possibilities of finding and holding love. He desired not only having the truth but seeing the reason why it was true by dispassionately probing for sources, causes and consequences. Thus Baldwin's deep concern was with one's past and the past of one's country or race as the starting point for understanding the present and foreseeing possible future developments.

Baldwin was, therefore, committed to exploring a wide spectrum of topics such as

> the responsibility of the writer to promote the evolution of the individual and society; the indivisibility of private life and the public life; the essential need to develop sexual and psychological consciousness and identity; the past historical significance and the current potential explosiveness of color consciousness and the racial crisis; the need for demythologizing the prevailing ethos of American history, religion, and culture; and the intertwining of love and power in the universal scheme of existence as well as in society's structures.[3]

He published six novels, two plays, eight books of essays, a Rap on race with Margaret Mead, a Dialogue with Nikki Giovanni, a book of short stories, a Collection of poems, a book for children, a film scenario based on the *The Autobiography of Malcolm X*, and a number of articles, interviews and book reviews in leading journals.

During the 1980's three major projects occupied him: a novel *Petals for Mohammed*, a play, *The Welcome Table* and a triple biography of the martyrs Medgar Evers, Malcolm X and Martin Luther King Jr., to which he gave the tentative title *Remember This House*.

It is interesting to note that Baldwin intended writing, in the early 1950's, a slave novel, set on the Emancipation Day in 1863, provisionally entitled *Talking at the Gates* in which he meant "to explore his belief that black and white in America were bound by strong ties, including blood ties, and that it was the pathological denial of these bonds, as opposed to actual differences, that fuelled the racial nightmare."[4] This indicates Baldwin's life-long commitment to work for racial integration in America.

When analyzed together his writings express his fundamental outlook and interests and there is a thematic homogeneity of his writings and the theme of commitment is a consistent and the most pervasive one in Baldwin's work, and it has shaped and dominated his life and art. Baldwin established a reputation as a man of letters and his prolific and provocative writings, so voluminous, so diverse, remain a revelation of his life and his commitments. "The great contribution of Mr. Baldwin is that he finds words to express what one knows to be true: how it feels to be an American Negro."[5]

James Baldwin had a singularly unhappy childhood. He was born in the year 1924 in Harlem. Harlem is "geographically part of the U.S., but sociologically an island surrounded by the rest of the country."[6] Berdis Emma Jones, his mother, who worked as a domestic servant married David Baldwin in 1927 when Baldwin was just three years old. David Baldwin was a sternly authoritarian religious fanatic who had migrated from New Orleans to New York. Young James thus acquired a name, a providing patron but not a benevolent father-figure. His illegitimacy obsessed him from the time he first learned about it in his boyhood right to the end of his life. He did not blame his mother in any way for bringing him into the world illegitimate; he was always very tender about her. He was a bastard child. He realized gradually why his father was rarely pleased with him. David Baldwin despised and taunted his stepson for his illegitimacy, his uncouth appearance and later, his independence of spirit.

His mother provided whatever compensatory affection she could, but her eight additional children born over the next sixteen years and her work in white people's kitchen left her little time to spend on her first born. In such a family situation, it is little wonder that Baldwin's major literary theme was quest for love and commitment. Love, for Baldwin, embodies the only redemptive power capable of helping man in defining his humanness. "You have lots of brothers and sisters" his mother used to say, "You don't know what's going to happen to them. So you're to treat *everybody* like your brothers and sisters. Love them."[7]

Baldwin's earliest years were a period of such unrelieved anguish that survival preoccupied him completely, delaying even recognition of the racial problem. His family life was emotionally depleting, economically deprived and socially oppressed like that of a host of Harlem families. The most that could be expected of such family was physical survival. The vicissitudes and vices of the neighbourhood in which the survival had to be achieved left an indelible impression on Baldwin's mind, first as evidence of the wages of sin, and later as the indicators of a racial bigotry. From such nightmarish reality, some escape was needed, some sustenance offering spiritual solace and physical safety and emotional release. For the blacks this solace was the storefront church where David Baldwin preached.

Baldwin found his solace in books. He'd sit at a table with a child in one hand and a book in the other. He steeped himself in literature:

devouring books as though they were ambrosia and for him, they were.

David Baldwin had eternal love for God as the major passion of his life, mercilessly, he strove to inculcate his faith in all the members of his family, not always with success. He was undoubtedly the most important influence on young Baldwin's life. It was from his father who played Jekyll and Hyde — a pious, peace-loving preacher on the pulpit and a lust-driven monster at home — that Baldwin acquired his detailed knowledge of the Bible, which was to affect his thinking and his style until he died. Baldwin learned that he was ugly which made him reserved and uncertain of himself for years. It was from his relationship with David Baldwin that he developed his obsession about rebelling against father-figures that was to make his relations with such veterans as Richard Wright so difficult. His stepfather's aggressive, often cruel dominance encouraged his homosexuality. He wished to rebel in every way. As he grew bigger, David Baldwin changed into someone to dread.

For James, religious faith was a ruse to protect himself from the dangers of the street, to placate his step-father, and finally to defeat him by excelling him in his own ministerial vocation. Whatever the motives, his intense emotional commitment to religion made James Baldwin an enduring literary luminary of religious subjects and imagery and a hortatory style, and high moral seriousness. His novels deal explicitly with religious experience and most of his writings derive titles or epigraphs from spirituals or scriptures.

School also relieved Baldwin from the stresses of home and enabled him to escape from his domineering stepfather. His diminutive size and precocity made him the easy target of schoolyard bullies; but his intellectual prowess helped to sustain him. A voracious reader, Baldwin read all the masterpieces and attempted to satiate his unquenchable thirst for knowledge.

He managed to overcome the difficulties of the actual world of home, street, church and school with the imaginary realm of book, play and film. He drew inspiration and encouragement from his teachers such as the poet Countee Cullen. Baldwin longed to become a writer. Before this ambition could be fulfilled, however, he had to confront sexual and religious crises, about which he has written at length in his novels. He could overcome the temptations of flesh only through a transcendent religious experience. It led him to the pulpit, where, as a boy-minister at the age of fourteen he could be the instrument of salvation for others. His histrionic gifts enabled him to outdo the more austere evangelical style of his stepfather. His popularity as a young preacher finally overwhelmed him. While his religious experience tentatively solved the moral issues of self, family and society his intellectual and literary development was complicating his sense of reality. As the voice of his skeptical, secular intelligence grew in volume, Baldwin's faith diminished. Leaving the pulpit and church, he was to become a ruthless critic of Christianity. The actual principles of the religious practices "were Blindness, Loneliness and Terror, the first principles necessarily and actively cultivated in order to deny the two others. I would love to believe that the principles were Faith, Hope and Charity."[8] The historical role of Christianity in legitimizing the ill-treatment of black people, as well as its stultifying effect on their lives, was to receive his bitter condemnation.

He lost faith in the Church; his family situation deteriorated, his father sank into madness, but his literary aspirations were still rising. He felt that he had to leave Harlem in order to survive. He secured employment as a defense worker in New Jersey. He found himself in an extremely hostile racial environment which seemed to confirm his stepfather's bottomless resentment of whites. He realized the dangers of being a black in America. This exposure produced a dread. His rage culminated in a violent confrontation in a Jim Crow diner in which he was ready to murder or be murdered.

Called back to New York because of his stepfather's fatal illness, Baldwin was now more prone to understand the role of white racism in shaping the black condition. On the day after the funeral, August 2, 1943, which was also Baldwin's 19th birthday, Harlem erupted in a riot occasioned by the shooting of a black serviceman by a white policeman. Baldwin had come to see in the riots the marks of racial oppression and discrimination.

He went to Greenwich Village to begin his career as a writer. Racial and sexual problems persisted, besides the problems of penury while he was undergoing his literary apprenticeship. However precariously, Baldwin managed to survive his years in the village and to make contacts that were to prove useful in his literary endeavours. He published a few book reviews for the *Nation* and the *New Leader.* In 1949, his most famous essay "Everybody's Protest Novel," denounced the use of fiction as a tool of social change. In his reviews of novels which dealt with racial protest he complained of over simplification and sentimentality about race.

Baldwin may be regarded as the first black American writer to alienate himself from the lone enduring black institution, the black church. He is known for his candid and persistent portrayal of its lack of authentic Christian commitment. He came to the conclusion that there was no love in the Church. To him religion was a mask for racial animosity and a shelter for despondency. The church that fails to save the body of a man from starvation can never redeem his soul from damnation. He concluded that he should abandon his connections with the church that was devoid of love and that looked like a house built on the rock of despair. The conception "that white man's God is White"[9] was inexorable, and the implications were clear. During the period of his early conversion, he wondered why, if white God loved all His children, the black children were rejected.

The problem further raises the question about why black people are religious, that is, Christian, in spite of the relatedness of Christianity to their enslavement. They yet stand in awe of God, whom they inherited from their God-fearing slave-owners. Baldwin says that "There are probably more churches in Harlem than in any other ghetto."[10]

Baldwin does not spare black church from his criticism. It too subtly but surely preaches hatred of whites. But his major attack is against white Christians, who so deliberately and shamelessly throw moral virtues to the winds to gain power and political leverage. Baldwin avers that the white Christian has robbed the African of his history and his religion. Baldwin believed that man, in order to become a truly moral human being must first free himself from all the prohibitions, crimes, and hypocrisies of the Christian church. He was convinced that the church should make us better, more loving toward all.

Baldwin recognized the distinction between sociology and aesthetics. He is thus among those black American writers for whom simple protest and anger were not enough. Baldwin condemned protest fiction in his essay "Everybody's Protest Novel" in which he found fault with the motives of Harriet Beecher Stowe and her opus *Uncle Tom's Cabin.* Baldwin denied that such writing can be justified on the basis that it serves the good of society. The novel employs biblical quotations, hymns, sermons and scriptural emblems and as a critic aptly put it, Stowe "rewrites the Bible as the story of a Negro slave."[11] Baldwin's view that *Uncle Tom's Cabin* combines the tradition of the sentimental novel and the rhetoric of antislavery polemic and that it is activated by a theological terror in which black equals with evil and white with grace is amply endorsed by Richard Yarborough who in his article entitled "Strategies of Black Characterization in *Uncle Tom's Cabin* and the Early Afro-American Novel" opines that "Although Stowe unquestionably sympathized with the slaves, her commitment to challenging the claim of black inferiority was frequently undermined by her own endorsement of racial stereotypes."[12]

Baldwin rejected overt racial conflict, though not race, as a literary theme.   When he was preparing his first major creative efforts, Baldwin met Richard Wright in 1945. Wright read his manuscript, praised his talent and helped Baldwin get a Eugene F. Saxton Memorial Trust Award, his first real literary recognition. Baldwin confessed that he looked upon Wright as a father-figure.

But, for Baldwin a father-figure was by definition what one rebelled against in order to establish one's own identity. He criticized Wright's famous works and rejected in his reviews of those books the Wrightian model of protest fiction.

Wright felt betrayed and Baldwin defended himself by saying that all literature may be protest but not all protest is literature.

In three essays particularly "Everybody's Protest Novel" (1949), "Many Thousands Gone" (1955) and "Alas, Poor Richard" (1962) Baldwin had openly acknowledged his affection for Wright, who became for him a "spiritual father." The anticipated relationship between the fledgling and the idol could not be sustained because of the deep and irreconcilable differences between their commitments. Two major points were responsible for the rupture: first, Wright's contention that Baldwin had "betrayed him and not only him but all American Negroes by attacking the idea of protest literature," and second, Baldwin's contention that Wright refused to accept "my right to my own vision, my right, as his equal, to disagree with him."[13]

In "Many Thousands Gone" Baldwin concentrates all of his rhetorical power in a massive attack on the validity of Wright's purpose in the creation of *Native Son*, with its monster protagonist Bigger. Although he admits that" the most powerful and celebrated statement we have yet had of what it means to be a black in America is unquestionably. Richard Wright's *Native Son*." (*N.N.S.* p. 30). Baldwin unfairly contends that at the end of the novel the readers know more about the monster Bigger than they did at the beginning and, likewise they know scarcely any thing new about the social condition which is supposed to have created him. Baldwin is sore about the fact that an important dimension of black life is omitted namely, "the relationship that Negroes bear to one another that depth of involvement and unspoken recognition of shared experience." (*N.N.S.* p. 35).

Wright's aim was to confront the readers with his protagonist Bigger created by the American republic and to make them share Bigger's experiences and to arouse in them the feelings of pity and horror at his inevitable doom.

Consistently adhering to the idea that the reality of man is more than a social reality and that the artist is rendered sterile who deals with man only in social terms, Baldwin has described Wright as a victim of the war between blackness and whiteness. Baldwin was of the opinion that Wright, when he died was acquiring a new tone, and a new depth and that in the collection of short stories *Eight Men* "Wright's unrelentingly bleak landscape was not merely that of the Deep South or of Chicago, but that of the world, of the human heart." (*N.K.M.N.* p. 149).

Baldwin was unaware in his early years of the necessity for various kinds of protest as a socially committed artist struggles to bring to life the compelling vision that his personal and social experiences offered. He was skeptical about Wright's relationship with other black Americans and on Wright's self-imposed exile. He accused Wright of arrogance and condescension toward blacks, of hypocrisy, of really not wanting to know the problems of his black country men in France, because, "his real impulse toward American Negroes, individually, was to despise them." (*N.K.M.N.*) p. 168).

Baldwin liked America too much to abandon it. He feared white Americans too much to live with them. He also like Wright, found exile as the only way available to him. "I left America because I doubted my ability to survive the fury of the color problems."

(*N.K.M.N.* p. 17). Baldwin suffered from a double alienation; as a black he could not see eye to eye with the white society that oppressed him and at the same time he could not identify with the black society. If he had been born in the south, he might have come to New York, but being born in New York, he had no place to go in America. He had to go out.

While on the continent, Baldwin was able to come to terms with himself and to reassess his own country, for which he has several times asserted his love. In cutting himself loose from America, he had hoped to obliterate the psychology of the outcast. It was in Europe that he became an American. He had to leave America in order to realize that he was part of it, or that it was a part of him. What became clear to him, as the result of his European exile, was the fact of his blackness and his Americanness. "I found myself, willy-nilly, alchemized into an American the moment I touched French soil." (*N.K.M.N.* p. 75).

As a writer, there was no way of escaping his role in a revolution. It demanded a great deal of stepping out of social situation in order to deal with it. And all the time he was out of it, he could not help feeling a little guilty that he was not, as it were, on the frontline, so he decided to terminate his self-imposed exile in France. He decided to stop indulging in elegant despair far removed from the scenes of racial conflict. As a committed artist he could not justifiably pontificate from a distance on the viciousness of racism while he kept himself comfortably protected form its immediate effects.

Go Tell It On the Mountain was published in 1953 to critical acclaim. Two more books *Notes of Native Son* and *Giovanni's Room* appeared before he returned to America to live in July 1957.

The Supreme Court decision of 1954 outlawed racial segregation in public education and at the end of the following year Dr. Martin Luther King Jr., launched a bus boycott in Alabama. Throughout the south, blacks were being brutalized at will and murdered with impunity as white racists rallied their forces in opposition to racial integration. Expatriation seemed to Baldwin an evasion of his social commitment.

Baldwin undertook an extensive tour of the south and met numerous leaders like Martin Luther King, Jr. Baldwin, through his essays, addressed mainly white Americans pleading fervently for their understanding support of the black struggle. He was recognized as a major spokesman of the Civil Rights crusade.

He became a genuine celebrity through his writings, lectures and plays and acquired name, fame and material prosperity. But Baldwin never lost his sense of racial outrage. He put American civilization to a merciless scrutiny with abiding faith in the healing power of love. The police violence and racial killings of many leaders including Martin Luther King Jr., had all but extinguished hope. And with this termination of hope came profound disillusionment and exile. Till his death in 1987 he had been commuting between Europe and America. "I love America more than any other country in the world, and, exactly, for this reason, I insist on the right to criticize her perpetually." (*N.N.S.* p. 9).

Baldwin claims the right to love America even though, she feeds him bread of bitterness. Despite all his years in Europe, he had never sounded like an expatriate. He realized that he had been an inseparable part of America, for better or worse, and did not belong to any other, not to Africa. He had no hesitation in asserting that "the black and the white, deeply need each other here if we are really to become a nation." (*T.F.N.T.* p. 83).

Baldwin was committed to exploring the quality of black suffering, to expose the racial and sexual polarization of his society and to challenge the readers to confront and resolve these aberrations. His writings "attest to his premise that the black American, as an object of suffering and abuse, represents a universal symbol of human conflict."[14] Baldwin, therefore, aimed at the portrayal of the black people's suffering in America. This portrayal is based on his own experience and the history of his people and their culture.

In order to fulfil this commitment the artist should be open-minded and aware of the experiences which appear to the common man both fragmented and chaotic. Baldwin thought that the artist is dedicated to a special vocation whose value never diminishes. This special task involves both personal and social responsibility. His subject is himself and he attempts to look on himself and the world as they are. The writer is also responsible to and for the social order, and his task must be pervaded by an ethical vision and historical orientation that includes "a responsibility, not only to ourselves and to our own time, but to those who are coming after us." (*N.K.M.N.* p. 189).

Baldwin pleads for a profound recognition and acceptance of the tragedy of life and to be truly alive is to be prepared to risk everything and to love is to be willing to give entirely of oneself. His commitment was to expose with candour and acerbity what it means to be black in a world dominated by white power in social, political, religious, artistic and ethical matters. His faith in remaking America into what it should be was unshakable. Not everything that is faced can be changed, but nothing can be changed until it is faced.

Baldwin grew up suffering hateful mistreatment, entrapment, exploitation and condescension and so he acquired the habit of referring to himself as though he were the personification of his race, embodying in himself the history, the attributes and the tragedy of the black American. He believed that the blacks are responsible for their freedom, and they are not begging for it, for freedom is not something that is given or granted, it should be taken or won. Freedom is unattainable since "freedom is discovery and recognition of limitations, one's own and that of one's society."[15] In the process of winning freedom one would have to hold in the mind forever two ideas which seemed to be in opposition. "The first idea was acceptance, the acceptance, totally without rancor, of life as it is, and men as they are: in the light of this idea ... injustice is a commonplace.... The second idea was of equal power: that one must never, in one's own life, accept these injustices as commonplace but must fight them with all one's strength." (*N.N.S.* p. 113-114).

The effort to become a great novelist "involves attempting to tell as much of the truth as one can bear, and then a little more."[16]

Commitments to these obligations compelled Baldwin to attack much that Americans tend to hold sacred in order to confront reality and to change it constructively. It meant devotion to "human being, his freedom and fulfillment; freedom which cannot be legislated, fulfillment which cannot be chartered." (*N.N.S.* p. 15).

When one is out of touch with oneself, one cannot touch others. Questions of self-discovery have tended for most other writers to be of more or less philosophical or aesthetic significance, the issue for Baldwin tended to assume enormity, since it has had everything to do with his very survival as a social being. The creative imagination for him seemed to be nothing but a vehicle of self-assertion in a world that conspired to deny meaning to his life.

Self-discovery is never an entirely private battle; it can be achieved only in communion with others. The bridge of suffering can enable one to define oneself through a committed, compassionate, and reciprocal understanding of the others. This idea of achieving self-discovery through recognition and acceptance of another's humanity is examined in Baldwin's novels. The capacity for communication with the commitment to another individual is the core element of genuine love.

Self-discovery is also dependent on identification of the individual self with group experience and tradition. Hence communal identification plays a crucial role in Baldwin's writings. He implies that for an individual to accept himself and develop a healthy ability to commune with another, he must come to terms with his racial past. The individual while strengthening the community, draws strength from it in turn. Thus an individual's quest for self-discovery and meaning ultimately involves a return to identification with and commitment to his community, his group tradition. He can achieve a genuine sense of self only through his identification with the humanity within all men and women. And in a real sense all of Baldwin's writings "constitute a magnificent assertion of the oneness of the human spirit that unites the family of mankind."[17]

Baldwin's novels deal with the impact on the individual of the conditions of urban life and society. He treats the anonymity, impersonality the confinement and isolation of the city life. The quest for community is indispensable in Baldwin's novels. This quest involves the discovery and the rejection of illusion about oneself, facing and fighting alienation and solitariness. Man is, after all, a gregarious animal. In order to define others and in order to relate with others he must reveal his interior being. For Baldwin the galvanizing force for overcoming the isolation is love. Baldwin's commitment to do away with racial segregation is to be seen in this light. Love is not an abstract spiritual entity. It is a life-sustaining force and an invigorating tonic to a suffering humanity. For Baldwin writing was an act of love and communion, symbolizing an attempt to get in touch with others and to get their attention and admiration. The only significant realities are individuals and love, and these individuals pursue love, and anything that hinders the free operation of this fact is evil. He adds that if "the concept of God has any validity or use, it can only be to make us larger, freer and more loving." (*T.F.N.T.* p. 46)

Racism may be seen as illustration of failure of love. If love is in part the willingness to accept the validity of another's life, so is racism, the denial of another's humanity. If love implies the ability to forgive, to be charitable, racial animosity is equally the inability to understand others and to be compassionate. Racism is a deadly battle which affects the victor and the victim alike. It is like a festering wound that must be worked upon until it is opened and the pus can run out. "It is like needling a blister until it bursts." (*N.N.S.* p. 59)

It is not easy to be a black in America. One is victimized from the start by the colour of one's skin. Society not only gives black people an inferior status but convinces them of their worthlessness. The stigma is stamped on the blackness of the Americans by the whites to rob the black men of their selfhood. From the beginning, white America has absolved itself of responsibility, by selfishly and cruelly clinging to the dictum: what is not white is inferior. "This is the crime of which I accuse my country and my countrymen and for which neither I nor time nor history will ever forgive them, they have destroyed and are destroying hundreds of thousands of lives and do not know it and do not want to know it." (*T.F.N.T.* p. 14)

One cannot live without a past, but the black is stripped off his past in America. A person or community which does not know its past and parentage is handicapped by an inferiority feeling. The full human potential is haunted by a rootless past. Hatred and fear of whites are concomitant to life for the blacks. They nurture hatred for their own group and self-hatred too. Baldwin confesses that he himself at one time despised black people. He was "as isolated from Negroes as I was from whites, which is what happens when a Negro begins, at bottom, to believe what white people say about him." (*N.K.M.N.* p. 17) A black child is taught in his school book that Africa had no history and that neither had he. It is not only that society thought of him as worthless and treated him as one, but that he himself believed it-that he never questioned what white people said of him. White America brainwashed itself into believing that the black really is intellectually inferior and sexually superior. It has convinced itself that the black American is happy in his place. But Baldwin was committed to expose America's systematic efforts to destroy blacks. It inculcates fear. In challenging the white world's assumption, the blacks put themselves in the path of destruction.

Baldwin declared that his most passionate concern-nay, obsession-was with race, "... that one problem is a problem which has obsessed my life. And I have the feeling that one problem, the problem of colour in this country, has always contained the key to all other problems."[18]

There is no one in the country better able to reach the conscience of America than Baldwin. Over and over again, he stressed the economic motives behind segregation and the commercial benefits white America derived from maintaining blacks as a source of cheap labour. Exploitations take place as a result of man's reluctance to face the truth about his own nature. This is a kind of myopia. Men erect an elaborate facade of myth, tradition and ritual and hide their true motives. It is this distorted vision which has created and perpetuated the vicious racism that threatens to destroy America.

Blacks grow up with a great wall built between themselves and whites and it makes whites strange, different, other. And whatever is "other" is frightening. The entire society reinforces this difference so that the blacks have to be afraid of the whites. And if they are afraid of the whites, the blacks have got to hate the whites. These restrictions and their effects are inexplicable and invisible whereas his skin is not. And it is his skin that predetermines the attitude of white strangers. His colour makes him simultaneously conspicuous and anonymous.

Baldwin was inspired by Mrs. Ayer, the principal of his school who made him believe, "that I was not necessarily what the country said I was."[19] But at the same time it was a white teacher who encouraged him and hence became for Baldwin "my first key, my first clue that white people were human."[20] Then he concluded that at the root of the American racial problem is the need of the white people to find a way of living with the blacks in order to be able to live with themselves. This realization of Baldwin did much to reduce the bitterness and tension in racial discourse and helped create a cordial atmosphere in racial relations. Along with Martin Luther King Jr., he helped shape the idealism upon which the civil-rights protest of the sixties was based. As a spokesman for his race, Baldwin found himself winning international reputation. Although committed to stress the cause of the blacks and his own outrage, he still remained an impartial human being. He was critical of both blacks and whites. He lamented that black people, "mainly look down or look up but do not look at each other, not at you, and white people, mainly look away." (*T.F.N.T.* pp.. 33-34)

Baldwin used the essay as his anvil for his fiction, both novels and short stories.

Go Tell It on the Mountain, Baldwin's first and his best novel, examines three generations of a black family whose life span extends from slavery to the present day. It is autobiographical and it is the story of a Harlem youth, John Grimes, who undergoes a religious experience on his fourteenth birthday. It narrates the story of John's stepfather Gabriel, a fanatical zealot whose power scars the lives of all who come near him. It is likewise the story of Florence, Gabriel's sister and of Elizabeth his present wife and John's mother. The various stories illuminate each other in their psychological intimacy. They also exemplify almost a century of black American social experience. The common denominators of the experience are sex, race and religion, precisely those elements with which John must contend with to achieve maturity and self-definition.

Gabriel refuses to accept or love John. Pampered and protected by his mother, John lavishes his love on her. Ridiculed and rejected by his stepfather, he reciprocates with fierce hatred. Symbolically emasculated by Gabriel, John turns to a slightly older, more virile youth, Elisha, for compensating affection, John ends up securing a homosexual surrogate. Thus, John's severe Oedipus complex propels him toward homosexuality.

John can achieve self-realization only when he accepts his blackness without associating it with ugliness, dirt and humiliation. Ashamed of his uncouth appearance, his colour, his ghetto environment, he has longed for the cleanliness and order of the white world. John's racial shame implies an indictment of the white racism responsible for it. On the threshing floor of the Temple of the Fire Baptized, John comes to a tentative racial self-acceptance when he hears a sound that come from darkness, the sound of the black past of suffering and victimization. He hears this sound, in the mood of religious transport. Reviled by his stepfather who thinks of John as the son of the bond woman and rejected because of the race by the country of which he is a native son, he turns to God. John's ecstatic moment is genuine, moving him through shame and hatred to love and peace. Yet all the implications of his commitments are that John will finally have to abandon religion to engage the world, just as he must leave the church to reenter the Harlem streets.

The search for self is presented mainly in sexual terms in *Giovanni's Room*, Baldwin's second novel. It is a book without the presence of a single black and it was among the first American novels to explore the subject of homosexuality with the same candour permitted for discussion of heterosexual love. The story is about two expatriate bisexuals David an American and Giovanni an Italian both living in Paris and David's girl friend Hella. David, loyal to his parents, keen to marry, start a family and launch a career, struggles with the questions of commitment. Having lost his mother when he was five, David suffers from a recurrent nightmare involving her. He was filled with shame and remorse at his father's drunken affairs with women. A brief, homosexual encounter with Joey compounds the confusion of the family situation. In an effort to find himself, David goes to France. There he meets Hella, an apprentice painter who leaves him to travel through Spain in order to evaluate their relationship, and Giovanni, working as a bartender at a homosexual resort presided over by Guillaume, a corrupt and shrewd scion of an aristocratic family. David moves into Giovanni's small, cluttered room; a genuine affection of their homosexual relationship is described vividly. His fear to commit himself fully to their love, constitutes a betrayal on David's part that drives Giovanni to desperation and finally to the murder of Guillaume. Apprehended, Giovanni awaits the guillotine while David, overwhelmed by guilt, strives to restore his relationship with Hella. David, who is inhibited by the social taboo of the love of one man for another is tormented by his own innate incapacity to accept love when he finds it. The action boils down to a choice confronting David: commitment to Giovanni he loves or compromise with Hella, his fiancé.

Heterosexuality a culturally sanctioned and socially prescribed pattern is accepted and commitments to human beings and to the deepest urgings of one's own nature are denied.

Another Country unfolds panoramic perspectives of New York city, where even the weather contributes to the human frailties and rattles the nerves with its relentless heat and noise, engendering hostilities and frustration. It is a place, run entirely for money, and by money. Its citizens seem to be robots. They appear to have no sense of their right to renew themselves. In such an environment the search for love of the major characters is destined to bear no fruits, since the reality of their lives is conditioned by betrayal and evasion and hatred and violence.

Another Country besides presenting its portrayal of a city, tells the interrelated lives of eight major characters. Rufus Scott, a black jazz musician fallen on evil days commits suicide, but his memory haunts the minds of his friends, most of whom consider themselves to be in some degree responsible for his untimely death.

The problems of Rufus arise from his uncommitted affair with Leona, a sincere, but indigent white refugee from the south whom he drives to a nervous break down. Vivaldo Moore a writer falls in love with Ida, the sister of Rufus. Ida a rising blues singer is a beautiful but embittered girl mourning her brother but determined to survive in the urban jungle by any means necessary. Richard and Cass Silenski are another oddly matched pair. In contrast with Vivaldo's efforts to write a meaningful work of fiction, Richard, his former teacher brings out an inept and worthless murder mystery. This literary prostitution costs Richard the respect of his wife, who admires Ida and Vivaldo. She then has an affair with Eric Jones, a homosexual, an actor who has recently returned from France leaving his male lover Yves, a Paris street-boy. Eric had earlier been involved homosexually with Rufus, and after Cass, he makes love to Vivaldo while waiting for Yves to join him in New York. Ellis, the T.V. magnate who promises to promote Ida's career, treats Ida like a whore.

The human craving for love and the difficulty of satisfying in the urban milieu is the theme of the novel. It amplifies the themes of *Giovanni's Room*, namely the healing power of love and the difficulty of accepting it. But there is a good deal more sex - interracial, extramarital, heterosexual, homosexual.

The failure to find a satisfactory affirmative answer drives Rufus to suicide, Leona to a mental asylum, Ida to the unloving arms of a television executive, Vivaldo to a delusion and to realize that their commitment to Rufus was not strong enough to save him from his suicide. Rufus who dies at the end of the first chapter, becomes a central figure for the other characters.

The novel is based on the assumption that the most tantalizing realities that the Americans have to deal with are race and sex. Each individual is an island, separated from others by race, sex or nationality. For any human being to reach out to another, sincere effort is necessary. The effort intensifies in direct proportion to the level of commitment. Ida, for example, is afraid to love black men as she has seen too many of them destroyed. But she cannot love white men either. Even her involvement with Vivaldo is to torment him.

The message of the novel is that blacks and whites must go to or create another country in order to regenerate the one they have. Since they cannot seek another country in Europe or Africa, it is America itself which is another country. They must look inward. Six of the major characters are artists. They must create harmony out of the ever present chaos of avarice, betrayal and perversion. Success attends where commitment reigns.

In the next novel *If Beale Street Could Talk*, Tish and Fonny, young black lovers are in conflict with a hostile urban society but are sustained by their love for each other. Falsely imprisoned on a charge of raping a Puerto Rican woman, Fonny must struggle to retain his sanity while Tish, a perfume sales assistant in a downtown shop, pregnant by him, struggles against time and a corrupt legal system to free her man before their child is born. In this effort she is supported by her parents and sister and Fonny's father, although Fonny's mother Mrs. Hunt and his sisters turn their backs on the trouble.

Fonny is a sensitive artist at odds with society. In the abrupt conclusion of the novel the baby has been born and Fonny is out on bail, although his legal fate is still uncertain. Nevertheless, life has been renewed through love despite all the malevolent forces of a corrupt and racist society. The affirmative conclusion is to be inferred.

For Mrs. Hunt church is a shelter and people like her are recluses who do not wish to face their problems. Baldwin indicts their apathy and disapproves the philosophy of waiting for the Lord's will to be done, their wallowing in guilt over imaginary crimes and their futile wailings. Tish's sister Ernestine like her parents is equally committed to saving Fonny. She provides a pleasant contrast to Adrienne and Sheila, who are Fonny's non-caring sisters. The good ones, altruistic and Christlike in their dedication and commitment deserve Baldwin's praise.

The coming together of Tish, Fonny, Tish's parents, sister and Fonny's father for commitment to and preservation of their love despite all obstacles, especially those represented by laws and courts presents an edifying spectacle in the novel. They symbolize the commitments of the individuals who have been wronged and believe that wrong can and should be righted.

Baldwin's attitudes have evolved from an effort at disengagement in his youth to fervent commitment to the redemptive power of inter-racial action for civil rights during 1950's to endorsement of black revolutionary nationalism during 1960's, to a bitterly pessimistic awaiting of retributive vengeance on the white racism of America that characterized his position in the 1970's and 1980's.

In *The Fire Next Time* Baldwin argues: Before blacks can be liberated from their condition, they must liberate whites from their racism by accepting them with love. Baldwin also sheds light on his youthful conversion, ministerial career, and rejection of Christianity because of the implausibility of its doctrines and the crimes committed in its name. He offers a report on his meeting in Chicago with the Honour-able Elijah Muhammed and a sympathetic assessment of the Black Muslims from a nonbeliever's point of view and an analysis of American racial relations in the context of national history and contemporary international politics. Baldwin's commitment as exemplified in this section is that black people are in a position to teach white people to give up their delusions of superiority and to confront the national political realities to eliminate racism as a necessary condition of survival. "If the blacks and whites do not end the racial nightmare and change the history of the world, the fulfill-ment of that prophecy, recreated from the Bible in song by a slave, is upon us: *God gave Noah the rainbow sign, No more water, the fire next time.*" (*T.F.N.T.* p. 89)

An even more emphatic endorsement of violence as a legitimate weapon of the racially oppressed appears in the novel *Tell Me How*

Long the Train's Been Gone. In the concluding scene of the novel the protagonist, Leo Proudhammer agrees, still somewhat reluctantly, with his friendlover Christopher, a black nationalist, that, however outnumbered, they require guns.

Whatever the particular circumstances, Leo's all-consuming emotion is fear, as he confesses to the reader many a time. Lying on his back in his dressing room after his heart attack, Leo realizes that his life revealed a very frightened man. In his childhood he was afraid of the friends of his brother Caleb. On the subways he first felt what may be called a civic terror. Leo realizes that terror and trouble are the two inseparable elements of his life's experiences. Such all pervasive fear coupled with bisexuality, the father-figure, the quest for love, and tirade against racism and loveless religion constitute the main plank of the novel.

Leo Proudhammer, a famous actor suffers a heart attack in the midst of his role one evening on a stage in a theatre in San Francisco. Accompanied by Barbara King, his white mistress and fellow-player, Proudhammer is rushed to a local hospital. Having recovered from his illness, he leaves the hospital, goes to New York and then to Europe to rest as well as to recuperate. Sometime afterward, he returns to America, resumes his work as an actor. The story is filled with a variety of episodes. The story is developed not by classical associationism, but by errant association-errant in that the connection between the various episodes is left for the reader to guess or supply for himself. The one thing all the episodes have in common is the protagonist's direct or indirect involvement in them, Proudhammer is thus the unifying force in the story and his commitment to his brother Caleb, to Barbara and to Christopher is the emotional centre of the novel.

The main character Arthur Montana in *Just Above My Head* is a gospel singer. His story is told by Hall, his elder brother. To remember Arthur is to remember Jimmy, Arthur's lover. And to remember Jimmy is to contemplate Julia, his older sister and a former child-preacher with whom Hall once had an affair.

Julia's mother Amy supports Julia's claim to the ministry as revealing her precocity. She begins to look up on Julia as a grounded angel. The problem is that Julia is not content to be the messenger of God, she is trying to play God and this brings a power that expects tolerance from others. She fails to save her mother because of her indifference. Two days after her mother is buried, her father, Joel, violates her.

Julia, the living example of transcending of the most excruciating kind of physical and emotional pain, that of incest, fascinates Hall by her ability to break the rules and to survive nonetheless. Uncertain about growing up, hesitant about her ministry and guilty about her mother's untimely death, she submits to her private purgatory.

In another ironic and incestuous twist, Julia is helped along the road to recovery by engaging in a sexual act with Crunch, who has been Arthur's first homosexual lover.

Julia is brought to the south to join her brother Jimmy. She takes up modelling and then makes a trip to Africa. She causes a destruction within her own family as long as she is fanatically involved in the church. It is only when she gives up the religion and tries to redefine religion in terms of secular commitment to family and friends that she is able to grow in ways that win approval from Hall, as well as from the readers too.

Contrary to the evasive attitude of other American writers towards a subject like incest, Baldwin is committed to deal with the taboo provocatively and to expose its pervasiveness.

The quest for love in the form of homosexuality, another taboo subject is explored in Baldwin's novels. His homosexual connections even with Dr. Martin Luther King Jr., is referred to by Baldwin's lawyer Theodre Kupferman, "I know of course, he was homosexual. Another writer who knew I was representing him told me he was known as 'Martin Luther Queen'".[21]

In all that Baldwin has written about homosexuality, there seems to be an implied plea without preaching, for the acceptance of homosexual persons by society. These abnormal, unfortunate, individuals are human beings, and should have their right to live their lives on an equal footing with other members of society. Baldwin attempts an artistic expression of this attitude by selecting homosexual characters as being just as suitable for fictional treatment as any other human beings.

Baldwin grew up convinced that he was ugly and was forever defensive about his appearance, eagerly seeking friendship at school and later sexual relationships as if to show that he was wanted, that he couldn't be that ugly if people were attracted to him.

In Baldwin's fiction there are a number of characters who are unable to establish relationships with their fathers, and who consequently reach out to other males for the kind of masculine love they were denied as children.

By identifying themselves with strong men they assume vicariously the masculinity they have missed in their family and social lives.

They become, momentarily at least, female in their quest for the masculinity that would provide them with identity. This becomes especially clear in the case of Baldwin, whose sexual and emotional development was dwarfed by a wrathful father and an oppressive society. Evangelical Christianity provided him with some sort of compensation. Since homosexuality is expressed in terms of physical attraction, John in *Go Tell It on the Mountain* apparently sins by trying to substitute Elisha for God. Homosexually is the medium through which he conveys his alienation from God and society.

Giovanni's Room, deals broadly with the sociological interpretation of sexual deviation and its repercussions. The treatment of homosexuality in the novel, seems provocative because of its apparent difference between received social standards of conduct and morality regarding homosexuality. Baldwin's stance is contradictory to commonly accepted norms in western society. His attitude towards homosexuality is unorthodox. The resolution of the plot of the novel itself contains Baldwin's ideas of the nature and character of homosexuality. The murder responsible for sending Giovanni to the guillotine takes place because David has deserted him. He abandons him out of his preference for a heterosexual relationship. David is acutely aware of moral imperatives arising out of his sense of masculine identity. David's commitment to Hella results in the abandonment of Giovanni.

For Baldwin homosexual love is the highest form of heresy he can conceive of. The body, the Bible tells us, is a temple consecrated to God. The body and worldly experience, properly understood, are instruments of grace. Giovanni knows this fact by intuition, but David learns it too late. The violation of innocence is not a vice, for it may lend meaning to one's humanity. It is also religious paradox of good emanating from evil. But here innocence is discovered in the relationship of men who have not yet been hampered by the concept of love as being exclusively hetero-sexual. For Baldwin it is only in homosexual love that innocence is experienced afresh.

In *Another Country* the homosexual relations may be thought of as an attempt to renounce the significance of engagement in sex, it occurs between blacks or between blacks and whites. For if homosexuality is seen as issuing partly as a result of a narcissistic desire to return to the self in search of sexual fulfillment, it is obvious that such a relationship is but a deliberate affirmation of the egocentric sexual principle.

A much tougher and more successful book is *No Name in the Street*, in which self-experience is juxtaposed with racial and social themes. Baldwin's self-exploration in this book is not to indulge in egocentricity but to explain the situations of other individuals, to provide a personal context for social analysis, and to add meaning to his historical judgements.

No Name in the Street shifts back and forth between past and present, between personal experience and public pronouncements. Here Baldwin is no longer urging his white readers to change their ways in order to avert the fire next time. No longer does he appeal to white liberals. There will be no moral appeals on his part to this country's moral conscience. His mode is embittered, pessimistic, sad, and somewhat tired. There is a terrible finality about his denunciations, dooming any hope of racial reconciliation in America.

Deeply affected by the assassination of Malcolm X, Baldwin had first planned to write a play based on the life of Malcolm X. He agreed to write a scenario for a Hollywood film on this subject, instead of a stage-play. Unable to adapt himself in southern California, and unable to compromise on the collaborative nature of writing for the movies and the specific changes in his script proposed by the producers, which he believed would seriously distort his sense of the meaning of Malcolm's life and death, he left Hollywood, and the film was never produced. Later Baldwin published the scenario as *One Day When I was Lost: A Scenario Based on Alex Haley's 'The Autobiography of Malcolm X'*.

In the book *Devil Finds Work* Baldwin took up the role of a film critic. His commitment was to preserve cultural values in films. Baldwin, in his childhood, found movie-going a means both of escaping from his stepfather's assaults on his personality and of coping with them. In the first section Baldwin relates the films he saw as a child to the issues of self and race, in the second section he analyses films dealing with race relations. He reveals the stereotypes, the unspoken assumptions, overt or covert racism, moral evasions, homosexuality and distortions of reality in films; in the third section, Baldwin offers an elaborate criticism of films like *Lady Sings the Blues* and *The Exorcist.* He viewed films as a vehicle of cultural expression and as an instrument of moral values rather than as mere artistic medium.

In all his writings Baldwin reveals himself to be an eloquent and passionately committed humanist. As a black writer he pleaded the cause of black, but at the same time as a man he devoted himself whole-heartedly to the cause of humanity. Baldwin startles one by his use of "We" because he speaks not as a black but as an American:" Our dehumanization of the Negro then is indivisible from our dehumanization of ourselves, the loss of our own identity is the price we pay for our annulment of his." (*N.N.S.* p. 25)

Baldwin's power as a writer lies in his ability to blend the deeply autobiographical with the political and social. He looked upon himself as the black Everyman. Hence his writing has a moral vigour.

Baldwin declared: "I wanted to prevent myself from becoming *merely* a Negro: or, even, merely a Negro writer." (*N.K.M.N.* p. 18) He conceded a decisive role to race, religion and nationality, but he has proved in no small measure that such determinants are deadly traps if they are not transcended. He was ultimately not concerned about race or nation "but about pain, commitment, about seeing and hearing, about honesty in relation to one's past, one's present and one's future as a person and as a people."[22]

For Baldwin writing was both an act of transcendence and love. It was an attempt to get the world's attention and an attempt to be loved. He saw that prejudice and hatred are recipes for ruin and reduce men to the level of animals and committed himself to keep his own heart free of hatred and despair. He worked towards the fulfillment of his dream of the humanity marching forward to that brave, new world where love and justice reign eternal and human beings can be different yet truly free. To achieve this Baldwin prescribes: "The obligation of any one who thinks of himself as responsible is to examine society and try to change it and to fight it-at no matter what risk. This is the only hope society has. This is the way societies change."[23]

It is necessary to consider the significance of Baldwin's writings beyond its value as sociological treatises. The bulk of the existing critical views is based on a social perspective and its attempt is to view Baldwin's writings as a means of justifying his role as the spokesman of the black Americans. No doubt his writings have tremendous impact on society. But equally important is his artistic achievements. An attempt to reveal Baldwin's commitments to art in discharging his duties as an interpreter, revelator and inspirer is the next logical step.

§ § §

NOTES

1.   *Contemporary Literary Criticism*, Vol. 50, p. 283.

2.   Granville Hicks, "Commitment without Compromise" *Saturday Review* (1st July 1961), p. 9.

3.   F. L. Standley and L. H. Pratt, op.cit., p. viii.

4.   James Campbell, *Talking at the Gates* (New York: Viking, 1991), p. 135.

5.   Stephen Spender, "James Baldwin: Voice of a Revolution," *Partisan Review,* 30 (Summer 1963), p. 260.

6.   Fern Marja Eckman, *The Furious Passage of James Baldwin* (New York:: M. Evans and Company, 1966), p. 11.

7.   Carolyn W. Sylvander, *James Baldwin* (New York: Frederick Ungar Publishing Co., 1980), p. 3.

8.   James Baldwin, *The Fire Next Time* (Harmondsworth, Middx: Penguin Books, 1963), pp. 34-35. Further references to this source will be abbreviated to *T.F.N.T.* and parenthesized in the text.

9.   James Baldwin, *Blues for Mister Charlie* (New York: Dial Press, 1964), p. 4. Further references to this source will be abbreviated to *B.C.* and parenthesized in the text.

10.   "The Harlem Ghetto" *Notes of a Native Son* (Boston: Beacon Press, 1955), p. 65. Further references to this source will be abbreviated to *N.N.S.* and parenthesized in the text.

11.   Jane Tompkins, *Sensational Designs: The Cultural Work of American Fiction 1790-1860* (New York: Oxford University Press, 1985), p. 127.

12.   Quoted in *New Essays on Uncle Tom's Cabin* ed. J. Sundquist (New York: Cambridge University Press, 1986), p. 47.

13.   James Baldwin, *Nobody Knows My Name* (New York: Dell Publishing Company, 1961) pp. 156, 159. Further references to this source will be abbreviated to *N.K.M.N.* and parenthesized in the text.

14.   *Contemporary Literary Criticism* Vol. 42, p. 13.

15.   James Baldwin, "An Interview" *WMFT Perspective*(December 1961), p. 37.

16.   James Baldwin, "As Much Truth as One Can Bear" *New York Times Book Review*(14 January 1962) p. 1.

17.   Emmanuel S. Nelson, "James Baldwin's Vision of Otherness and Community.", *Melus* 10, No. 2 (1983), pp. 27-31.

18.   Margaret Mead and James Baldwin, *A Rap on Race*(Philadelphia: J. B. Lippincott Co., 1971), p. 69.

19.   "James Baldwin Talks with Kenneth Clark", *The Negro Protest* (Boston: Beacon Press, 1963), pp. 6-7.

20.   William J. Weatherby, *Squaring Off: Mailer Vs. Baldwin* (New York: Mason Charter, 1977), p. 24.

21.   W. J. Weatherby, *James Baldwin: Artist on Fire - A Portrait* (New York: Donald I. Fine, 1989), p. 169.

22.   Carolyn W. Sylvander, op.cit., p. 149.

23.   James Baldwin, *The Price of the Ticket: Collected Nonfiction 1948-85* (New York: St. Martin's/Marek, 1985), p. 326. Further references to this source will be abbreviated to *The Price* and parenthesized in the text.

CHAPTER FOUR

JAMES BALDWIN - PART TWO

In his writings James Baldwin displays the nature of his own specifically artistic quest which includes the search for the real and the development of his personality as an artist. He impresses the readers by his powerful, moving and ennobling account of the nature and development of his extraordinary soul. He describes his struggle against the perverted human contexts in which he grew up. His experiences vividly explain what sources of strengths were needed to protect his own individuality, innate talents, and his humanity from dissipation and degeneration. His dilemma was "essentially that which has always faced that artist who is also, consciously or not, committed to a specific social problem".[1] Baldwin endeavours through his art to express the enduring truth of human experience. The quest for the real takes its birth in a drive which pushes one into the depth of ordinary, everyday occurrences and opens out to the extra-ordinary dimensions of life; it unveils the real, which is to be found in and through the essential core of one's experience.

Baldwin aimed at demonstrating a certain competence in dealing artistically with the raw material of his experiences; his commitment was to see his aesthetic and social responsibilities as constituting a whole that does not discard the meaning of his experience and his desire to express this in an artistically satisfying way. To him the development of a purposeful public voice was as essential as the formulation of an artistic vision of life. With his experiences Baldwin accomplished "the only real concern of the artist, to recreate out of the disorder of life that order which is art." (*N.N.S.* p. 7).

This quest first turns inward in order to perceive one's own potentialities and limitations and steps outward toward the others in the society and understanding their past. Accepting "one's past - one's history - is not the same thing as drowning in it, it is learning how to use it." (*T.F.N.T.* p. 111).

Central to Baldwin's essays is his concept and use of history. The inability to face one's history means a lack of maturity and "until we excavate our history, we will never know who we are."[2] Baldwin is of the view that the black is ill-treated in America because history is written in the colour of his skin. This is the central fact in the history of America. No matter how much he must suffer in America, no matter how much he fears and hates the torture house into which he is cast, Baldwin realizes that, he must live in America. It is only after his return from Europe when he makes his odyssey to the south that he is able to appreciate the positive results, the strength and beauty of the people who have suffered slavery and the most appalling social and economic inequities.

Whether one believes every sordid details of Baldwin's particular experiences or not, his portrait of black life in general impresses the readers as true. Baldwin does not exaggerate the dread, despair and depravity of the lives of the blacks in America. Through his artistic portrayal Baldwin makes the readers wonder what sort of commitment and strength could have overcome the forces seeking to knock him down.

Protest literature, Baldwin argues, is false because it seeks to deny man's freedom; and its murky sentimentality, and the tendency to offer the facile explanation of man as a social being devoid of all complexity are the defects of such literature.

Protest fiction and the naturalistic novel treat man as a simple product of biological and environmental determinism. They deny the possibility of escape from these external forces.

Fantasy and escapism are unknown elements in the actual lives of black people, but the literature that presents and interprets their life is firmly rooted in realism. The black writer seeks to present a picture of experience and also attempts to re-order the chaos of reality.

All art may be seen as protest by virtue of its commitment on the one hand to offer mechanical reproduction of reality and on the other to suggest a *radical revision* of that reality. Baldwin's views on the hidden truth of the protest novel are well-known. Far from being a tool for liberation, the protest novel merely perpetuates the false image of blackness, an image that the white American cherishes. Baldwin explains the psychological necessity for the white man to construct an image of black inferiority and to hold this image between himself and the truth. Paradoxically, the image reflects not black reality but white guilt.

Baldwin in his fiction presents his characters with their faults and strength, as full human beings, not as propagandistic caricatures of good and evil. He has recognized the danger to artistic and realistic rendering of character that are presented with an intention of propaganda. He was committed to present his characters without minimizing their faults or extrapolating their virtues.

His writings may serve as a powerful weapon in a just cause, but the fact that it is essentially a protest does not deter him from telling the story of his own soul. His writings besides telling the story of the development of his personality as an artist, reveals what his life may have in common with the lives of others. It shows how Baldwin is moulded, through a struggle with stifling and hostile forces and gives the meaning of his artistic endeavours and achievements.

The efforts of Baldwin to protect himself against the violence of oppressive white society and the corrupt and pervasive forces of the ghetto life are vividly delineated. Normally, the powers of a black man are allowed to dissipate in a self-consuming way, whether he knows his place and retains it or drowns his desires in drugs and sex. At times he releases his rancor in crimes of wanton destruction and mindless violence, or in religious frenzy. But Baldwin is not destroyed in his attempt to withstand the pernicious forces; he learns to endure, he is even tempered by them. The meaning of his blackness is contained in having endured these forces. All his powers are concentrated and converted into creative and transformative fire.

This struggle to revive and nurture the positive human qualities is led by the struggle to feel and record human suffering and hurt. To feel and to be hurt is a necessary condition for meaningful and committed action on behalf of others in pain. Pain and suffering are universal themes in literature, if art is a criticism of life. The most authentic quality of the black writer's life is not alienation, certainly not the complacency of affluence, but a seemingly inescapable hurt. His commitment is to record this hurt and while doing this he has to retain sanity and to keep his feet firmly upon the ground of his unique experience.

As he records his hurt, he conceives himself as an artist. Baldwin thinks of his art as a high calling for his commitment is to the human race and his responsibility is to the future.

He sees all about him moral bankruptcy and raises the cry of what to do to save the world. He confronts the sordid facts of American life and attempts at an imaginative grasp of the complex aspects of the human conditions, and a creative perspective on future possibilities. He sees the object as in itself it really is. To do this demands a disinterestedness that is especially difficult for Baldwin. Rage sometimes overpowers, and hate gets the upper hand. Baldwin is convinced that "the artist ... cannot allow any consideration to supersede his responsibility to reveal all that he can possibly discover concerning the mystery of the human being"[3] and that the ultimate concern of the writer is "to examine attitudes, to go beneath the surface, to tap the source." (*N.N.S.* p. 6). This implies that the role of the artist is to present the real life experience to others. The artist corrects the distortions to which the society falls a prey in its efforts to avoid this knowledge. The artist explores and expresses an adequate perspective of the disturbing complexity of the people and enables them to discover the power that will free them from their foibles and illusions.

He is convinced that Americans must take an honest look at themselves and their country, especially in their dealings with the blacks. He warns the whites to mend their ways to avert their doomsday and look objectively at themselves and at others so that they can perceive who and what they are.

The artist cannot and must not take anything for granted. Therefore the writer's duty as artist imposes on him the role of a warrior. The exercise of such responsibility by the artist involves risks and requires extraordinary power and dedication. The society isolates its artists for their vision and penalizes them. This is not the artist's fault, though the artist will have to take the initiative in changing this state of affairs. "One is always in the position of having to decide between amputation and gangrene." (*N.N.S.* p. 112). Amputation means restructuring and gangrene means allowing the *status quo* to continue. "Baldwin's language from his first writings has been distinguished, precise, well-ordered, very sophisticated, it could describe extreme experiences with chill casualness, and apparently trivial experiences with a simple but effective use of extreme language that conveyed the underlying importance of the apparently trivial."[4]

One can change the situation, even though it may seem impossible. To accomplish this task one must be influenced by wholesome forces. Baldwin's influences were the King James Bible, the rhetoric of the store-front church, something ironic and violent and perpetually understated in black speech. "My models -my private models- are not Hemingway, not Faulkner, not Dos Passos, or indeed any American writer. I model myself on jazz musicians, dancers, a couple of whores and a few junkies...".[5]

Baldwin's autobiographical intimacy with such materials required and received artistic skill and distance. Baldwin created fiction that transcended racial and religious categories and became an evoked image of man facing the inscrutable universal forces.

Baldwin examines closely his own experience through his art. He never attempts to ignore his blackness. He acknowledges both the sweet and bitter influences that have shaped his life and art. Neither does he base his artistic motivation upon the desire to escape his blackness. He would like to transcend or obliterate all structures, stereotypes, superstitions, whether they are imposed by white men or set up, defensively, by blacks.

Evidently, Baldwin wishes to reduce the importance of his blackness, not because of the shame which he has been forced to feel but rather because in emphasizing this essential fact, he is that much further alienated from his perceived ideal of himself as a human being and artist. Perhaps he sees that being a black man in America tends to frustrate the achievement of the emotional distance necessary to artistic creation.

The unique feature of his style is his tendency to relate his personal life and experiences with whatever commentary he offers on social and moral questions. His caustic comments on social realities evolve directly from his personal experiences. He, therefore, speaks with an authority. His astonishing flow of high eloquence is denounced by critics as speechmaker's prose. "Baldwin seems to have lost respect for the novel as a form, and his great facility with language serves only to ease his violations of literary strictness".[6]

Like Baldwin's stepfather, Johnny, the protagonist of *Go Tell It on the Mountain* was an incongruous mixture of piety and cruelty.

"Everyone had always said that John would be a preacher when he grew up, just like his father."[7] But Johnny, like Baldwin, "would not be like his father, or his father's fathers. He would have another life". (*Go Tell* p. 18). Baldwin committed himself to be a writer. This eventually made him famous.

Baldwin had always been as much a preacher as a writer. In his style, there remained the atmosphere of the pulpit. In his works a sublime rhetoric rushes out, as in a sermon. Baldwin includes a number of sermons in his novels and short stories.

The profession of preaching served as a launching pad for Baldwin to enter the realm of literature. The synthesis of down-to-earth parables and biblical examples is an exercise for anyone who wishes to master the technique of writing fiction. His prose has rhythm, and an irresistible charm of the evangelical oratory. Gabriel Grimes' sermon, for example, blends logic and passion and becomes at once rational and emotive:

> For let us remember that the wages of sin is death; that it is written, and cannot fail, the soul that sinneth, it shall die. Let us remember that we are born in sin, in sin did our mothers conceive us - sin reigns in all our members, sin is the foul heart's natural liquid, sin looks out of the eye, amen, and leads to lust, sin is in the hearing of the ear, and leads to folly, sin sits on the tongue, and leads to murder. Yes! Sin is the only heritage of the natural man, sin bequeathed us by our natural father, that fallen Adam, whose apple sickens and will sicken all generations living, and generations yet unborn! It was sin that drove the son of the morning out of Heaven, sin that drove Adam out of Eden, sin that caused Cain to slay his brother, sin that built the tower of Babel, sin that caused the fire to fall on

Sodom - sin, from the very foundations of the world,
living and breathing in the heart of man, that causes
women to bring forth their children in agony and
darkness, bows down the backs of men with terrible
labor, keeps the empty belly empty, keeps the table
bare, sends our children dressed in rags out into the
whorehouses and dance halls of the world!

Amen! Amen! (*Go Tell* p. 116).

The subject of his sermons is invariably the life that blacks live, but his
real audience is white America, in spite of the fact that his following
among black Americans is large and loyal. He committed himself to
be the messiah of the maltreated and therefore his words are aimed at
those whom he thought as their tormentors. He also imbibed a sense
of theological terror engendered by man's unequal relationship to the
Heavenly Father rather than his equal relationship to his brethren,
both black and white.

This sermonic style of the black ministry is ideally suited for personal
testimony, for the conveyance of faith, passion and commitment. *Go
Tell It on the Mountain* is saturated with a religious perspective
drawing from the Christian tradition. The entire text is peppered with
scriptural references, allusions, images, symbols, names, concepts and
rituals. The title of the work is derived from a combination of the
Christian plantation song, "Go Tell It on the Mountain" and
scriptural passages from the Old Testament. The novel's epigraph is
also derived from the same sources. Each of the three sections of the
novel, both in sub-title and epigraph, is drawn from Biblical sources.

A study of Baldwin's use of irony and sly teasing reveals his artistic
distance from the characters and his attitude toward their religious
beliefs. The narrative technique as used by Baldwin reveals an
internal and subjective point of view limited to the thought, feelings
and perceptions of Johnny. Baldwin uses irony of statement and

event in the action and ironic voice on the whole as a character.
Johnny "wanted to obey the voice, which was the only voice that
spoke to him; ... only the ironic voice insisted yet once more that he
rise from that filthy floor if he did not want to become like all the
other niggers." (*Go Tell* p. 220). Although Johnny speaks in the third
person, the point of view is strictly maintained, so that even the
physical appearance of the hero is described subjectively through
comments he hears from others and the images he sees in the mirror.
The readers follow Johnny through the course of his fourteenth
birthday, as if they were experiencing the events with him.

Baldwin's excellent command of language and his penchant for poetic
expression are used to present the thoughts of a Harlem Youth
without restriction to his grammar and vocabulary. Baldwin's ear for
language and his skill at representing it in print are demonstrated
throughout the novel. The subtlety, accent and rhythm of black
vernacular English can be experienced in all Baldwin's fiction. The
contrast between the narrators' diction and the dialogue of the
characters emphasizes both the universality of their inner conflicts and
the particular circumstances of their lives as blacks in America.

Baldwin introduces verbal irony when he describes human motives in
terms of divine providence or when he uses Biblical allusions to imply
an action contrary to the meaning of Biblical context. For example,
the description about Gabriel and Deborah when they were going to
be married informs the readers:

> She, who had been the living proof and witness of
> their daily shame, and who had become their holy
> fool - and he, who had been the untamable despoiler
> of their daughters, and thief of their women, their
> walking prince of darkness! And he smiled, watch-
> ing the elders' well-fed faces and their grinding jaws -
> unholy pastors all, unfaithful stewards; he prayed
> that he would never be so fat, or so lascivious, but

that God should work through him a mighty work:
to ring, it might be, through ages yet unborn, as
sweet, solemn, mighty proof of His everlasting love
and mercy. (*Go Tell* p. 123).

Gabriel employs Biblical quotations to terrify his congregation and to
assert his own righteousness. "'Set thine house in order', said his
father 'for thou shalt die and not live'" (*Go Tell* p. 222). The first
mention of this text is placed just after the breakfast scene, which
reveals the disordered condition of Gabriel's house and his unhealthy
family relationships. A second mention of the text suggests that
Gabriel is unaware of his own approaching death.

Deeply rooted in the social realist tradition, Baldwin's *Another
Country* (1962) examines the lives of a group of young Americans at
a specific period in history. "Talk about art vs. propaganda. *Another
Country* was almost nothing but propaganda; propaganda for
homosexuality."[8] The prose is, in places, clumsy. Baldwin instead of
portraying the characters like an artist, explains like a spokesman.
The novelist and the essayist alternately appear throughout the novel.

The novel *Tell Me How Long the Train's been Gone* (1968) is long,
but the main effect of its size is to display its faults in abundance. The
narrative is presented largely in the form of flashbacks, the language
is uninventive. The opinionated voice of the essayist intrudes into the
novel. The protagonist Leo's voice is in fine, Baldwin's voice.

Leo, his parents, and Caleb his elder brother are involved in the
various episodes. Through experiences of these people, the reader
witnesses some of the circumstances and shocks to which Harlem life
is heir. Life in apartment houses, juvenile delinquency, crime, police
brutality and the evils of racism are dealt with. The quality of
coherence in the story is affected because the various episodes that
appear to be flashbacks prove to be reminiscences embedded in other
reminiscences.

Baldwin took the bold step of making the narrative voice of *If Beale Street Could Talk* (1974) female. In trying to endow the female narrator Tish with a depth of wisdom and a vocabulary which should have been beyond her capabilities, Baldwin only does her harm, for he deprives her, a character of her own.

The hallmarks of black vernacular English are its rich ironic wit, poetic double-edge, and rhetorical 'rapping'. They are abundantly displayed by Langston Hughes in his Simple sketches. But Tish, a Harlem girl conveys her thought through an analytic literary medium. This raises the charge that Baldwin has misrepresented and undersold black speech.

One can learn the special features of black speech by going through *Little Man, Little Man* such as "He about the color of chocolate cake without no icing on it. Except when he grin, but he don't really never grin, except at TJ and sometime he act like he don't see him," "Them eye-glasses blinking just like the sun was hitting you in the eye", "This street long, It real long", "TJ more like he in a jungle where he can't get no satisfaction", "But she ain't no boy"[9] and so on.

Just Above My Head (1979) contains too many characters, too many long-winding conversations and descriptions, too many rhetorical passages and too much of authorial intrusions. Unlike Tish who tells her own story, Julia has no narrative voice, her life and passions are revealed through the male psyche of Hall. The novel is replete with flashback technique.

Baldwin came into contact with a number of artists, both black and white, who were to be major influences on him. Beauford Delaney, a painter, was credited with teaching Baldwin how to see clearly everything with an artist's point of view and how to trust what he saw and to question the meaning of what he saw. Baldwin has dedicated his books to some of his artist-friends. For example, he dedicated his book of short stories *Going to Meet the Man* to Beauford Delaney.

It is interesting to note that many of the Baldwin's heroes are artists by profession, men whose deep sensibility unveils them to the evils of their community and allows them a perception whereby they come up with proper responses.

It is by no means a necessary and sufficient condition of success that the responsibility of the artist should end with the lyric expression of frustration and anger. Ultimately, Leo's final declaration of commitment at the end of *Tell Me How Long the Train's Been Gone* must be seen as an eloquent indication of Baldwin's advocacy of a new perspective on life. Leo's commitment to the politics of active confrontation indicates Baldwin's belief in the essential worth of man and the responsibility of the artists.

Music and measure lend grace to human personality. It is very important to realize that music, like all art regardless of its form, is ideological. It reflects or transmits certain political, class and national interests. A creative and revolutionary music, however, is more than just reflective, but criticizes the very social mosaic of the society, and ultimately contributes towards giving shape to the reconstruction of that society. Black music is the most socially conscious music. It has been the music called the blues and the jazz. They reveal the realities of self, society, nation and race to their practitioners and listeners. They comfort the people in their hours of pain and encourage them to fulfil their commitments.

The profound suffering revealed in blues music especially in the music of Bessie Smith, seems to have special significance for Baldwin himself if one is to believe that the most moving and effective art is autobiographical. Baldwin fled to Europe and in Switzerland he discovered his identity as an American. "There, in that absolutely alabaster landscape, armed with two Bessie Smith records and a typewriter, I began to recreate the life that I had first known as a child and from which I had spent so many years in flight". (*N.K.M.N.* p. 18). The blues must have had for Baldwin some meaning associated with the fundamental experiences that mould one's personality. They had a special significance for Baldwin since they connected him with his blackness, his Americanness, and with that which makes him an individual. The blues are laconic and mellifluous. They are deliberately realistic, and they unfold the sordid details of living.

Like A. Murray, Baldwin seems to consider that "the whole point of the blues idiom is to state the facts of life.... the ugliness and meanness inherent in the human condition. It is thus a device for making the best of a bad situation".[10] To communicate one's feelings through the blues, one must be frank and upright and one must also have suffered intensely. Only those who have undergone suffering and have triumphed over their torments can understand the message of the blues and can communicate to other sufferers through their music. In the short story "Sonny's Blues", the hero's particular sufferings are his own, but he communes with others through his music. This proves that music unites all the sufferers. The blues music is a sedative both for the singer and his audience. It offers a timely relief from the pains of their daily realities.

The blues seemed a natural vehicle in which to express Baldwin's ideas. For incidents in his own life had many similarities to the contents of many blues lyrics: (a) early desertion by the man in his life, for Baldwin was an illegitimate child, (b) continued search for love, extreme poverty, hunger, and white racism, (c) perseverance to overcome the difficulties and (d) the message as to how the others can survive in a racist society.

Like the blues, Baldwin's writings proclaim that there is something vitally wrong with this world. Traditionally, singing the blues symbolized the meaninglessness of the pains of the black people and artistically expressed it in words blended with music. It offered the blacks a certain distance from their pains and allowed them to view their pains artistically. That the blacks could master pains without bye-passing meant that they were not subdued by them.

This commitment to survival against odds is persistent in Baldwin's writings. Baldwin through his writings, like blues singer attempted to teach and to delight, to strengthen and to pull his people together as they stand and serve inspite of the meanness inherent in the human condition.

"The blues are an attempt to retain the memory of pain, to transcend catastrophe, not by taking thought -- for that often only adds to the pain -- but by an attitude a nearly comic, nearly tragic lyricism."[11]

Only when one is honest about the particulars of one's own experience can one become stronger because of those experiences; likewise, only when one recognizes the universality of human suffering can one profit from the particular sorrows of others.

The title of the book *Go Tell It on the Mountain* is from a black spiritual:

> "Go Tell it on the mountain,
> Over the hills and everywhere;
> Go Tell it on the Mountain,
> that Jesus Christ is born."

Earlier tentative titles of the book were "Crying Holy" and "In My Father's House" and "The Birth". The last title chosen suggests the new birth of John represented in his conversion at the end of the book.

Throughout *Another Country* Baldwin refers to blues and the great jazz musicians such as W. C. Handy in the epigraph, Fats Walter, Charlie Parker, Bessie Smith and Billie Holiday. His intention was to show that these musicians have tremendous social significance.

The title *If Beale Street Could Talk* is a line from an old W. C. Handy[12] blues. Though Beale street actually offered few opportunities for success to blacks, it grew to fame as the birth-place of the American blues. It is both the evil effect of racism and the value of the blues as a tool of survival that Baldwin is attempting to depict in this novel. The weak and the meek eventually succumb to the racist system, while those who have faith in God and break their bonds through blues and by extension, through other forms of creative expression are able to survive.

> *"Didn't my Lord deliver Daniel? And why not every man?*
>
> The song is old, the question unanswered."[13]

Just Above My Head, the title, is the first line of the song that Ida Scott, the black jazz singer sings in *Another Country:*

> "Just Above My Head
> I hear music in the air
> And I really do believe
> There's a God somewhere."[14]

The joy comes only out of pain and examination of pain. The resolution comes only out of confrontation of pain. *Just Above My Head* is a gospel tale told in the blues mode. The history of the blacks is in the "sorrow songs" -- gospel, blues and jazz.

In the play *The Amen Corner* gospel hymns are used. They are precursors of the blues as a tool for black survival. As in the earlier black spirituals, the image of heaven served to liberate the black mind. Blacks were able to transcend the difficulties of today and to live as if the future had already come. This faith enables one to gloss over the facts of one's own life, it is an escapism that permits one to avoid facing the truth, and acts as a mere ruse for survival. It is only after abandoning the escapist beliefs that one can confront one's failures and frustrations and only then is one fit to sing the blues and to rise above one's despondency.

Baldwin shows Sister Margaret in *The Amen Corner* as maturing from being over-dependent on God and gospel hymns to relying on herself and other blacks and the blues for survival. She has learned the truth from Luke when he advised her son, David: "Son don't try to get away from the things that hurt you. The things that hurt you - sometimes that's all you get. You got to learn to live with those things and use them:[15] Baldwin's commitment was to show the effect of the blues music and how it enables the blacks to face life's pains honestly, seriously and optimistically, with a strong determination to survive.

Sister Margaret is a dynamic leader of her flock, but she is fanatical and tyrannical. Like Gabriel Grimes, she advises others to "set thine house in order," yet her house is in fearful disorder; her son is in the process of leaving the church for more mundane pleasures; her dying husband has returned home, after a long separation, to enable her to face the consequences of her choices; and even her hold on her congregation is slipping.

Margaret tries to escape the pain of living in the world by embracing a religious faith that has nothing to do with love. Denying her function as a woman, she has turned from her husband's arms to the sexual surrogate of religious fervour. Religion is shown betraying the primary relationship as Margaret advises a young woman to leave her husband, as she had done the better to serve God. Betrayed by her followers, scorned by her husband Luke and disappointed by her son David, Margaret in her very defeat, manages to gain a clarity of vision that constitutes a kind of triumph. To love God is to love all His children and suffer with them and rejoice with them and never count the cost. Even in the midst of suffering and frustration "You realize that your suffering does not isolate you; your suffering is your bridge".[16]

Blues for Mr. Charlie constitutes another effort by Baldwin to force white America to confront the plague of race. In his prefatory note

Baldwin speaks of the necessity to understand even the most unregenerate white, who is after all a product of the national ethos. He may be beyond liberation, but we can "begin working toward the liberation of his children." (*B.C.* p. xiv). Baldwin makes it clear that "All white men are Mister Charlie" (*B.C.* p. 40).

Based on the Emmett Till case of 1955, the play treats the racial murder of Richard Henry, a young black man returned home after living in the north, by Lyle Britten, a white store-owner. The murder scene is presented in full at the end of the play, after Lyle has been found innocent of the crime by a racist court. Within this frame Baldwin explores various aspects of racial life and relationships in "Plaguetown". "The play then for me, takes place in Plaguetown, U.S.A., now. The plague is race, the plague is the concept of Christianity" (*B.C.* p. XV). In probing the causes and effects of racism, Baldwin finds the sexual motive to be its core.

Richard is a jazz musician. Like Rufus in *Another Country*, he attempts to achieve racial revenge through contacts with white women. He is proud and sensitive and tormented, too rebellious to survive anywhere in America. Richard's specific torment originated in his reaction to the death of his mother, whom he believes to have been murdered by white men for resisting their sexual advances, and his shame at his father's acquiescence.

After experiencing white racism, he has reached the conclusion that the only way black men can achieve power is by picking up the gun. To pacify his grandmother, he gives his own gun to his father, leaving himself unarmed for the fatal encounter with Lyle. This surrender of the gun, shows his recklessness. He goes to the store run by Lyle. In the course of his conversation with Josephine Gladys Britten, Lyle's wife, Richard teases her. He also mocks at Lyle telling him that he is impotent. The sexual insult is repeated just before Lyle fires his first shot, and the dying Richard accuses Lyle not only of sexual jealousy of him but also of homosexual interest in him. Lyle's violence proceeds directly from the vicious combination of sex and race. Even Jo complains of Lyle's uxoriousness and hints at his infidelity. His past affairs include his clandestine relationship with a black woman whose jealous husband he murdered.

At the end of the play, Parnell James, the white liberal requests Juanita, "Can I walk with you?" (*B.C.* p. 121) and marches alongside the blacks symbolizing his determination to commit himself to the cause of blacks. The play ends with a note of optimism.

To Baldwin the theatre and the pulpit are one and the same. "When I entered the church, I ceased going to the theatre. It took me a while to realize that I was working in one."[17] Later he abandoned the church and preferred the theatre.

Richard's father, a black preacher says, "You know, for us, it all began with the Bible and the gun. Maybe it will end with the Bible and the gun" (*B.C.* p. 120). He puts Richard's gun in the pulpit, under the Bible. Baldwin's life too began with the Bible but did not end with the gun because he committed himself to the theatre, to art and to the positive power of love.

The title story of Baldwin's collection of short stories "Going to Meet the Man", presents Jesse, a white police officer, who wants to make love to his wife but is unable to do so. He lies in bed, and recollects a lynching that he witnessed when he was a boy. It tells the readers about the castration and burning of a black man. The readers can feel the action taking place in their presence. One almost hears the howls of the black victim and smells his burning flesh. Baldwin, once again, succeeds in his commitment to portray the relationship between race and sexuality, between white guilt and black anguish.

In his short stories, Baldwin begins by creating a situation, goes on to introduce a conflict or complication and concludes with a resolution of the conflict. "Sonny's Blues" is the most perfectly realized story.

There is nothing wasted in the story. It moves from situation to situation. Sonny, like the other artist-protagonists of Baldwin's novels, is the artist-in-exile. He is out of step with mainstream society. He marches to the beat of his own drum. He will eventually develop into Rufus or Richard of Baldwin's other works.

Like Rufus and Richard, Sonny in "Sonny's Blues" is a musician. He is not able to secure the emotional support he needs from his family. Unlike Rufus, Sonny becomes a dope-addict rather than committing suicide in response to his suffering. Through musical expression he transmutes his own suffering and that of his family. Thus he redeems himself and expands his elder brother's moral awareness.

The story is narrated by Sonny's brother, a conventional, middle class black man who teaches in a Harlem High School. He keeps himself aloof from the pain surrounding him. He comes to know of Sonny's arrest on a heroin charge. He also learns more about his brother through a friend of Sonny's. The very way in which he learns of Sonny's trouble is a measure of his failure to be his brother's keeper. This, precisely, was the charge imposed by his mother. Love and support were necessary to save one another from the pervasive darkness or to enable one another to survive it. He recollects his mother's advice: "You got to hold on to your brother," she said, "and don't let him fall, no matter what it looks like is happening to him..."[18]

After the death of their parents, he has to look after Sonny. He cannot reconcile Sonny's commitment to jazz. His daughter, Gracie's death from polio stirs the feelings of his own vulnerability. He is forced to renew his contacts with Sonny. His pain made him realize Sonny's pain. It is this commitment to love and to share the sufferings of others that constitutes the theme of "Sonny's Blues". Baldwin's message is as basic as it is undeniable. If we do not love one another we will destroy one another.

Baldwin's experience as a minister and a playwright is so vigorously applied to his prose style. Role-playing, folk-story telling techniques, repetition for intensity, rhythm and rhetorical flourishes of the sermonic style are found in Baldwin's prose. Baldwin employs these stylistic features of preaching for secular purposes. Instead of redemption in the eyes of God, Baldwin is committed to the redemption in the eyes of men. God is replaced by love for humanity and morality.

It is relevant to note here that Stowe presented Tom in her *Uncle Tom's Cabin* as pious, patient and timid. He is murdered by Simon Legree for refusing to betray his escaped fellow slaves, Cassy and Emmeline and for refusing to capitulate to Legree's demand that he renounce his Christian beliefs. His death results from his aggressive non-violence and Stowe's representation of Tom as the Christ-figure. Besides Tom, Stowe's typical Christ-figure is Eva, the book's most powerful evangelist. These characters direct the reader's sympathies away from the issue of slavery into sentimental feelings. Stowe adopted the sentimental mode in the presumption that emotion is superior to reason, and sensibility to logical ratiocination. Baldwin disapproved sentimentality, emotional exaggeration and the implicit argument that persistent purity ultimately overcomes vice. He was for the novel of sensibility which allowed one to feel deeply about any situation without having compunctions that something must be done to rectify it.

In Baldwin's fiction characters, especially women characters, progress from trying to secure sanctuary in the church to realizing that it offers none. In their lives, "Community replaces church, and secular, social commitment replaces traditional religion and the hope of heaven."[19] Baldwin's women always mean business, they do not wait passively for things to happen, they act. "To act is to be committed, and to be committed is to be in danger." (*T.F.N.T.* p. 17). Society offers no protection to these women, they are thrust into a world hostile to their very existence. Baldwin's women study and evaluate circumstances, choose their own destinies in spite of the pressures of family and society. Baldwin's portrayal transcends race and colour. Through the portrayal of Leona, Cass and Barbara all white women and Florence, Ida, Tish and Juanita all black women, Baldwin proves that the function of a woman is not just to keep a house clean and bed warm. Baldwin's women possess amazing insight, startling depth of compassion and commitment.

Toni Morrison, a black woman writer praises Baldwin thus:

> You made American English honest-genuinely international. You exposed its secrets and reshaped it until it was truly modern, dialogic, representative, humane. You stripped it of ease and false comfort and fake innocence and evasion and hypocrisy. And in place of deviousness, clarity. In place of soft plump lies was a lean, targeted power. In place of intellectual disingenuousness and what you called "exasperating egocentricity," you gave us undecorated truth. You replaced lumbering platitudes with an upright elegance..... In your hands language was handsome again. In your hands neither bloodless nor bloody, and yet alive.[20]

Baldwin's words can be angry, sarcastic and apocalyptic but they are always urgent, intended to egg on the readers to realize the gravity of the explosive situation in America and to stimulate them to take appropriate timely action. His major thrust is not to impart knowledge but to provoke and to propound eternal truths in order to alleviate human suffering. "Whether or not the United States is a place where persuasion and example can undo the injustices of which Mr. Baldwin speaks, we shall know within a matter of years. It is certain that only years, not generations, are left in which the injustices can be undone."[21]

The obligation of bestowing universal understanding on human motive and action invariably remains to be performed by the artist. The concept of commitment may include the notion of risk to expose. When the artist witnesses and exposes the realities of existence, the society may not like to be exposed since the society finds such exposure embarrassing. "It is for this reason that all societies have battled with that incorrigible disturber of the peace-the artist.... The artist cannot and must not take anything for granted, but must drive to the heart of every answer and expose the question the answer hides." (*The Price* p. 316).

The artist finds himself intensely alone in his moments of creation. But this experience of aloneness, in no way prevents him from involving himself actively in political or social affairs. Detachment is essential for the sake of maintaining an independent and impartial perspective. Money, fame and blind acceptance by the society might place the artist in a precariously tight spot where his power of discernment is in peril. The artist must overcome these temptations. "Baldwin has served as a spokesman for the artistic conscience in its struggle with its Black inheritance, in its aspiration to a human estate."[22]

Baldwin's voice sought to reason with the white Americans even as it exposed their equivocation and evasion. He appealed to the decent and humane in the whites, he tried to make them realize that a real egalitarian society served the interests of the humanity of all hues. *The Fire Next Time* announced the threat about the fire next time. At the same time it stressed the virtues of love and brotherhood as a *sine quo non* for averting the imminent disaster. Like the protagonist of one of his short stories, Baldwin realized that "hatred had corrupted me like cancer in the bone." Peter, the protagonist of the story "Previous Condition" is a young actor. He finds it difficult to identify with the black or the white society. This difficulty represents the source of his alienation as a black in the white society and as an artist-intellectual in his own society. When he returns to Harlem and takes a drink in a bar there, he muses: "But there was nothing except my color. A white outsider coming in would have seen a young Negro drinking in a Negro bar, perfectly in his element, in his place, as the saying goes. But the people here knew differently as I did. I didn't seem to have a place." The last portion of this musing and Peter's answer to his friend Jules earlier, "No room at the inn"[23] may be juxtaposed with the answer that the parents of Jesus Christ got at Bethlehem. The artists are always kept out of the society, irrespective of their race or colour.

The artist functions as a social palliative and corrective. He alone is capable of striking a balance between the image of Americans both black and white with the truth about them which they try to evade. He is committed to disturb the complacency of the people and to prepare them to deal with the calamity. His objectivity enables him to perceive the realities and to illuminate the defects of the society. "In its sensitivity to shades of discrimination and moral shape, and in its commitment - despite everything - to America, his voice was comparable in importance to that of any person of letters from recent decades...".[24]

To call Baldwin a black writer, then, is to condemn him to a literary ghetto; it is to disengage him from his testimony. Despite all his experiences, despite all that has been done to him, his response is not a literature delineating the barrenness in which so many Americans wallow. He responds with abundant love and unwavering commitment. The objects of his love and commitment are blacks, America and the humanity as a whole.

There are adverse criticisms too, of Baldwin's writings. Eldridge Cleaver condemned:

> There is in James Baldwin's work the most grueling, agonizing, total hatred of the blacks, particularly of himself, and the most shameful, fanatical, fawning,

sycophantic love of the whites... He becomes a
white man in a black body. A self-willed, automated
slave, he becomes the white man's most valuable
tool in oppressing the blacks.[25]

Baldwin, like Goldsmith's Village Schoolmaster mesmerized his
contemporaries with "words of learned length and thundering voice."[26]
His writings urged both blacks and whites to abandon their cherished
illusions and face their experience. He freed himself as artist from the
distortion of propaganda, the threat of self-pity or violence. The
techniques used by Baldwin enabled him to have control over his
material, to imprint form on vagueness and to create a prose order
which moves by revealing the organic relationship between experience
and expression and to give birth to an inescapable artistic unity.

Time is the best arbiter and Time alone can pass a verdict, favourable
or otherwise, on the value and meaningfulness of Baldwin's life. His
writings, like those of other writers must be vindicated by the posterity
in order to evaluate the commitments of his works and judge the
artistic excellence which will outlive the social value of his artistry.

According to Baldwin, Ralph Ellison "is the first Negro novelist I
have ever read to utilize in language, and brilliantly, some of the
ambiguity and irony of Negro life". (*N.N.S.* p. 9). As a corollary to
the analysis of Baldwin's life and writings, it is interesting to have an
in-depth study of the commitments and achievements of Ralph
Ellison, a distinguished contemporary of James Baldwin.

§ § §

NOTES

1.   C. W. E. Bigsby, *Confrontation and Commitment: A Study of Contemporary American Drama 1959-66* (London: MacGibbon and Kee, 1967), p. 126.

2.   M. Preston, ed. "The Image: Three Views," *Opera News* (8 December 1962), p. 10.

3.   "The Creative Dilemma", *Saturday Review* (8 February 1964), p. 15.

4.   John Thompson, "Baldwin: The Prophet As Artist", *Commentary* (June 1968), p. 67.

5.   Fern Marja Eckman, op. cit., p. 242.

6.   Irving Howe, "James Baldwin: At Ease in Apocalypse", *Harper's Magazine*, 237, No. 1420 (September 1968), pp. 95-100.

7.   James Baldwin, *Go Tell It on the Mountain* (New York: Dial Press, 1963), p. 9. Further references to this source will be abbreviated to *Go Tell* and parenthesized in the text.

8.   Calvin C. Hernton, "A Fiery Baptism", in *James Baldwin: A Collection of Critical Essays* ed. Keneth Kinnamon, (Englewood Cliffs, New Jersey: Prentice Hall, 1974), p. 114.

9.   James Baldwin, *Little Man, Little Man: A Story of Childhood* (New York: Dial Press, 1976), pp. 7, 10, 14, 30 and 33.

10.   Albert Murray, *The Hero and the Blues*, The Paul Anthony Brick Lectures, Ninth Series (Columbia, Mo.:   Univ. of Missouri Press, 1973), p. 36.

11.   Joseph Featherstone, "Blues for Mister Baldwin", *New Republic*, 153 (1965), p. 34.

12.   W. C. Handy, "Beale Street Blues", *Blues: An Anthology* (New York: Macmillan, 1972), pp. 116-19.

13.   James Baldwin, *If Beale Street Could Talk* (New York: Dial Press, 1974), p. 106.

14.   James Baldwin, *Another Country* (New York: Dial Press, 1962), p. 313.

15.   James Baldwin, *The Amen Corner* (New York: Dial Press, 1968), pp. 41-42.

16.   James Baldwin with Nikki Giovanni, *A Dialogue* (Philadelphia: Lippincott, 1973), p. 74.

17.   James Baldwin, *The Devil Finds Work* (New York: Dial Press, 1970), p. 29.

18.   James Baldwin, "Sonny's Blues", *Going to Meet the Man* (New York: Dial Press, 1965), p. 118.

19.   Trudier Harris, *Black Women in the Fiction of James Baldwin* (Knoxville: University of Tennessee Press, 1985), p. 11.

20.   Toni Morrison, "Life in His Language", *The New York Times Book Review* (20 December 1987), p. 27.

21.   Dan Jacobson, "James Baldwin As Spokesman", *Commentary* (December 1961), p. 502.

22.   Ihab Hassan, *Contemporary American Literature 1945-1972* (New York: Frederick Ungar Pub. Co., 1973), p. 75.

23.   James Baldwin, "Previous Condition", *Going to Meet the Man* (New York: Dial Press, 1965), pp. 94, 100 and 92.

24.   "James Baldwin", *The Norton Anthology of American Literature* Vol. 2., ed. Nina Baym et. al., (New York: Norton and Co., 1989), p. 2109.

25.   Eldridge Cleaver, "Notes on a Native Son" in Keneth Kinnamon ed. *James Baldwin: A Collection of Critical Essays* (Englewood Cliffs, N.J.: Prentice Hall, 1974), pp. 67, 70.

26.   Oliver Goldsmith, "The Deserted Village", 1.213.

CHAPTER FIVE

RALPH ELLISON - PART ONE

With the publication of *Invisible Man* in 1952, Ralph Waldo Ellison moved into the front ranks of American writers. He had already published ten short stories and thirty seven essays on literature and social problems. His second novel is yet to see the light of the day. He has published twelve short stories since *Invisible Man* and two books of essays *Shadow and Act* (1964) and *Going to the Territory* (1986).

The character of the artist in Ellison's nonfiction corresponds to the portrait of the protagonist of *Invisible Man*. One can discern the evolution of a central theme in all his writings: the more conscious a person is of his personal, racial, national and cultural heritage, the more committed he becomes. Ellison was not interested in documentary and protest fiction which delineated characters struggling to survive the quintessentially American environment and yet eventually getting defeated by irrational forces. Protest novels represent black life inordinately dreary, they are more sociological than literary. He wanted to depict the infinite possibilities and richness of life in which human beings are able to understand their environment and master it by force of character, commitment and positive action and the role which individual skill and excellence can play in charting changes within society.

Though Ellison has virtually "disappeared" after his epoch-making novel, he continues to operate, in a sense, invisibly to fulfil his life-long commitment to serve the noble cause of cultural pluralism and artistic integrity and the distinctive richness and beauty of black American life. He insists upon the variety, ambiguity, comedy, and tragedy of human life throughout the world. As a writer Ellison's commitment was to charge one's work with as much life and truth as possible. He viewed freedom not simply in terms of necessity but in terms of possibility. He is forever committed to the idea that art is a celebration of human life and not a woebegone wailing about social ills.

Ellison has sought to capture in his writings the language and lore, the rites and the values, the mirth and the miseries, as well as the variegated nature of black life in America. According to him the only way to understand universal values and patterns is to hold fast to particularities of time, place, culture and race. His *Invisible Man*, is no doubt the story of a black American, but his experience is so deeply human that readers throughout the world identify and sympathize with him. "It was as though my novel has become a lens through which readers of widely differing backgrounds were able to see elements of their own experience brought to a unifying focus".[1]

For Ellison the task of the novelist is to achieve for himself and for his readers some new insight into the human predicament, some new facet of human possibility. The novel is basically a form of communication of a vision of life and experiences of a specific man or society. If the novelist is successful, the specific experience he dealt with in his work will speak metaphorically for the whole and help to form its readers' sense of humanity and conception of eternal values.

The specific complex of experience is the life of black Americans. Novelists seldom conceived black characters possessing the full, complex ambiguity of the human and the tendency to distort or to stereotype black Americans was not peculiar to novelists only, it could be seen in other subjects too. Ellison decided that he would not ignore the racial dimensions at all, but he would put them into a human perspective.

So Ellison committed himself to the depiction of characters in his writings as possessing the full complex ambiguity of the human and the sweep and variety of the black American experience from the days of slavery to Emancipation and to the present and the black's perpetual alienation in his native land.

Ellison exploited the oral tradition and the narrative technique as employed by slaves and their descendants in the autobiographies and fictional life - histories in his writings.

For Ellison, folklore and rituals are essential to the understanding and to the depiction of the genuine nature of his people and "it is one of the functions of the artist to recognize them and raise them to the level of art".[2] Hence Ellison committed himself to the use of these motifs in his writings. Jazz, blues, signifying, spirituals, worksongs, boasts and a host of other distinctive forms of black American creative expression provided perspective to what he depicted in his writings. He also felt that black American "folklore is very powerful, wonderful, and universal. And it became so by expressing a people who were assertive, eclectic and irreverent before all the oral and written literature that came within its grasp." (*G.T.* p. 283)

Ellison believed in the autonomy of black culture within a pluralistic American context, so his commitment was to express his own position as a black American writer in relation to the inescapable white culture without forgetting his indebtedness to the masterminds of the western literature for their insight, influence, examples, ideals and techniques and for the tradition of American humour with its liberating potential.

Ellison's central commitment is with individuality and the efflorescence of human personality even in a hostile and sterile environment. In exploring the lower depths of human personality, Ellison poses questions about the nature of reality, the limits of human possibility and the meaning of social responsibility.

These questions are probed with a missionary zeal in *Invisible Man* which presents itself as an epic statement of the need for black self-definition.   The protagonist, a representative black American discovers himself when he gives up the definition of reality supplied by others.

The basic image of the novel is withdrawal from humanity and the basic strategy is the presentation of the experiences of a nameless protagonist. He is both anonymous and invisible because the civilized world has chosen to ignore him.

"I am invisible, understand, simply because people refuse to see me".[3] He addresses the reader in the first person and deals in paradox, ambiguity and in jest. He discovers himself the healing power of love and of human fraternity and declares that "there's a possibility that even an invisible man has a socially responsible role to play". (*I.M.* p. 439).

The Prologue of the novel finds the protagonist in a cell in the basement of a building rented strictly to whites. He pilfers light from the Monopolated Light and Power Company. Light gives form to his invisibility and this is essential to him because people refuse to see him as he really is. He remains for the present in a state of contemplation, recalling from the past, events which have led him to his invisibility.

The narrator of the story goes through a number of rites of initiation. He enters each stage of his life confidently and is eased out of it callously. The first of these is an episode from his adolescence, about the time of his graduation from high school. He is invited to address a white businessmen's smoker. There he is forced to take part in an obscene ritual: a group of black boys are confronted with a naked blonde and threatened equally if they ogle at her and if they avert their eyes. This is followed by a *Battle Royal* in which the boys are thrust blindfolded into a boxing ring and forced to fight one another. Then they are compelled to retrieve their prize money from an electrified rug. The prizes of white society in the form of women and money are tantalizingly held out to the blacks, only to be denied.

In spite of this degradation and swallowing of his blood, the boy, who nurtures dreams of becoming a leader of his community, delivers his prepared speech. As a reward he receives a scholarship to a black college, along with a briefcase.

The next few chapters are about an incident which occurs in his junior year and results in his expulsion from his college. Assigned as a chauffeur to one of the visiting white trustees, Mr. Norton, he inadvertently commits the sin of taking him into a slave quarters near the college campus. Mr. Norton meets Trueblood who narrates his own story with humour, delicacy and horror. He has brought disgrace to the black community by having fathered his daughter's child. He explains the conditions that gave rise to the incest. He has committed the very sin that Norton has impotently coveted. He does what Norton cannot do. Although others ostracize and sneer at him, his white neighbours treat him as something of a local celebrity. They lavish upon his infamy, material benefits which they have always offered grudgingly to his industry. Norton, whose incestuous attachment to his own daughter has been moved by the Trueblood episode, acknowledges his kinship with chaos by a gift of a hundred dollars.

Severely shaken, Mr. Norton requests a stimulant and the protagonist drives him to a bar called the *Golden Day.* Unfortunately, it is the day when the inmates of a nearby veteran's hospital pay their weekly visit to the local prostitutes. Once more Mr. Norton encounters chaos.

In the light of Trueblood and the Golden Day, the irony of the southern black college is revealed. Its function is not to educate but to indoctrinate with a myth. This myth is presented in all its splendour in the college chapel address of the Reverend Homer Barbee. It is only towards the end of this speech that the protagonist realizes that Homer Barbee is blind.

Dr. Bledsoe, the president of the college, is a harsh task master and a pragmatist who holds his own in a ruthless power struggle by cynical methods. He suspends the youth, but obliges him by giving him letters of recommendation so that he can seek employment in the north. He furnishes the youth with letters of introduction to several wealthy patrons of the college.

The youth leaves for New York and meets the white patrons. He receives only evasive answers from his prospective employers. He realizes that he has been not just rusticated but expelled, and discovers that Bledsoe's letters contain instructions to keep him running.

The protagonist is then hired as an unskilled labourer in the Liberty paint factory. He is put to work on a batch of paint which is needed for a national monument. He is asked to measure ten drops of a black liquid into each bucket of "Optic White" and stir until the black becomes invisible. Unfortunately he takes his refill from the wrong tank and mixes the paint with concentrated remover. By rendering visible that which is black, he unknowingly exposes the secret of the national whitewash.

The youth is hired so that the company will not have to pay regular union wages. He goes to work for a "slave driver" named Kimbro, who introduces him to the regimentation and fundamental irresponsibility of factory life. Soon he is sent to the basement to work for a black foreman, Brockway who represents the skilled black labour force. Borckway has made himself indispensable, for it is he who mixes the base of the paint, and yet he lives in constant dread of being replaced by whites. For this reason he is an Uncle Tom, a loyal servant of the whites who is fanatically anti-union.

The protagonist is caught between Brockway and the union, for each party suspects him of harbouring sympathies for the other. His first act of rebellion against the system occurs in this context, and he attacks Brockway, the black underling. In the course of a quarrel with Brockway, they forget to check the pressure gauges.   An explosion occurs and the youth finds himself in the factory hospital, a part of his personality obliterated.

The hospital scene is symbolic of the protagonist's rebirth, i.e., his new life in the *Brotherhood.* Only half conscious, he is tied to a strange machine and subjected to a shock therapy.   The atmosphere of antiseptic efficiency, of coldness and impersonality, of helplessness and passivity of the hospital evokes a symbol of modern mechanical life.   The protagonist is asked to think of his name, and those of his parents.   When he fails to remember, thus relinquishing all claims to individuality, he is declared cured.

The protagonist's personal fate in the Brotherhood, a clear version of the Communist Party, is the representative of a whole generation of black intellectual, who resists the "insistence upon blind discipline" and "constant pressure to follow unthinking a political line" (*G.T.* p. 209).

After leading a spontaneous demonstration against an eviction, he is recruited by the Brotherhood and thereby he finds a new identity.   He is initiated into the mysteries of the dialectic of Brother Jack, and assigned to agitational work in Harlem.   When a mass movement begins to develop, the policy of the Brotherhood shifts its emphasis from local to international issues, and the Harlem problem is sidetracked.   The protagonist is in a dilemma whether to betray the black people or to break with the Brotherhood and to go into political oblivion.   He decides to give up his association with the party.

In an organization which is ready to sacrifice the individual on the altar of history, the protagonist remains as invisible as ever.   His loss of individuality is felt most keenly when his sense of commitment collides with the discipline of the party.   He is always reminded of his black heritage and encouraged to work for it.   He is also warned against the dangers of black chauvinism and offered all the inducements of universal brotherhood. This represents a conflict between assimilationism and Black Nationalism. He regards the giving up of his folk tradition as some sort of moral victory. But this is self-effacement and it is discarded. He surrenders to the pleasures of a new sense of freedom and self-acceptance by embracing black folk heritage.

His racial ties are slightly weakened when he gets a glimpse of the possibility of being more than a member of race in the party. But he cannot shed his old skin so easily. The Sambo doll and the leg shackle presented by Brother Tarp remind him of his links to his racial past.

Ras the Destroyer, a black nationalist, is a West Indian agitator modelled upon Marcus Garvey. In an attempt to drive the Brother-hood out of Harlem, he engages the protagonist and his chief lieutenant Tod Cliffton, in a savage street fight. Pleading the case for Black Nationalism Ras chides the blacks for enslaving themselves to the white world.

To escape two followers of Ras, the protagonist wearing glasses with lenses so dark that they appear black and a white hat that he is immediately mistaken for Rinehart, the flamboyant gambler and the pimp, the innocent rapist and the briber, the shrewd number runner and the "Spiritual technologist", who is, in fine, an eternal breeder of crimes and deft manipulator of chaos. He personifies the fragile charms of vice and delectable wickedness. His middle name is Proteus. He is the symbol of escape and possibility. Invisible Man realizes that by impersonating Rinehart just a bit, he can overcome the problems of being himself and enjoy the benefits of being some one else. In the guise of Rinehart he exploits Sybil, a white woman. A frantic telephone call urges him to return to Harlem where a full scale rampage has erupted. Invisible Man heads for Harlem and joins a group of men who loot a store and then set fire to a tenement building.

Invisible Man realizes that the Brotherhood had planned the riot to liquidate Ras.

Pursued by vigilantés the protagonist drops through a manhole into a coal cellar.

After the narrator's fall into the coal pit he discovers that his arrogantly naive construction of personality is nothing more than the accumulated fragments in his briefcase, the high-school diploma, Bledsoe's letter, Clifton's Sambo doll, Mary's bank and Brother Tarp's iron. Those artifacts represent not him but the world's variegated projections of him. He decides to share his experiences with others.

"When he retreats underground to write his own story, he commits himself to sifting through those experiences and attributing his own meaning to them".[4]

The Epilogue picks up the tonal patterns of the Prologue, implies that meaning has been discovered and commitment has been fulfilled, and forces a direct connection between the narrator and the reader.

The criticism that Ellison's *Invisible Man* received was copious and varied. According to Saul Bellow who was lavish in his praise, *Invisible Man* is a book of the very first order, a super book which displayed "the very strongest sort of creative intelligence."[5]

> Langston Hughes finds *Invisible Man* to be "deep, beautifully written, provocative and moving" (*New York Age*, 28 February 1953). Both Henry Winslow (*Crisis*, June-July 1952) and Alain Locke in a more extensive essay (*Phylon*, 1953), praise the novel's artistic qualities, and above all, its psychological realism, depth and skillful irony. They also point out to the same defects, aptly summed up in Locke's

words as "hyperbole and verbosity". Nevertheless, Locke unequivocally declares the novel "to mark the third peak in the development of Negro fiction (following upon '*Cane*, 1923 and *Native Son*, 1940)."[6]

Kerry McSweeney quotes Richard Chase describing the novel as "the search of an innocent hero for knowledge of reality, self and society." (*Kenyon Review*, 14, 1952), John Killen's review,: "It is a vicious distortion of Negro life.," (*Freedom*, 1952) and the *Daily Worker* (1 June 1952) "In effect, it is 439 pages of contempt for humanity, written in an affected, pretentious, and other worldly style to suit the king-pins of world white supremacy."[7]

Howe, a left-wing Jewish literary intellectual, insisted that to write simply about 'Negro experience' with the aesthetic distance urged by the critics of the fifties, is a moral and psychological impossibility, for plight and protest are inseparable from that experience. "If *Native Son* was marred by the ideological delusions of the thirties, *Invisible Man* was marred (albeit 'less grossly') by those of the fifties."[8]

Indeed, the bulk of the adverse reviews directly contradicts Granville Hick's assertion that "the day *Invisible Man* appeared, American culture was changed forever."[9]

J. Noel Heermance isolates two major innovations of Ellison in the tradition of the black Novel: (1) his "harsh and frank description" of the roles available to blacks within the "cage of white society" and (2) "his use of the black culture to show how these roles may be transcended."[10] *New York Herald Tribune Book Week's* poll[11] taken in September 1965, asked 200 authors, critics and editors to assess the fiction of the twenty-year period 1945-65. Ellison ranked sixth in response to the question as to what authors had written the most distinguished fiction, but *Invisible Man* topped the list of the "20 best books" of the period.

In order to understand why such extreme views are expressed about Ellison's writings, it is necessary to examine his personal, social, racial, literary and artistic commitments and how Ellison fulfills them in his works. His novel should be considered as one might consider any other written work of art, and it should also be considered within the context of sociological issues including the problem of self-image for a minority group struggling to achieve genuine acceptance.

Ellison confesses: "Let me say right now that my book [Invisible Man] is not an autobiographical work" (*S.A.* p. 167). But a number of similarities between the life experiences of the protagonist and the author may be cited to treat the novel as a "simulated autobiography."[12]

At a time when many writers are committed to the registration of the tremors of the self's experience, of its own inwardness in an adverse world, Ellison's focus is on the self, but on the self at that point where it encounters a significant social reality.

The society treats the black American as an alien and denies his existence by simply ignoring him. He presents a paradox; the blackman, being most visible, is most invisible; most easily seen, he is least comprehended.

The individual's sense of his own existence depends upon confirmation of his being, by others. This sense of being is developed in early infancy. It is an inner assurance. Some persons lack this and they operate from a position of insecurity and such persons engage in a series of maneuvers designed to reassure them of their own existence. Reality is perceived as extra-ordinarily threatening and they dread relationships with others. When a man's true self, as he perceives it, is never recognized and confirmed by others and when other's perception of him never squares with his self-concept, he can justly doubt his existence. He is treated either as "boy" or as "uncle" never as a "man". He is a "non-man". He has become invisible. He has no name; others use him only to confirm their own selected fiction. He is acted upon, never an actor in his own right. He is instructed: "Just do what you're told and don't try to think about it". (*I.M.* p. 152) and reminded by the Brotherhood: "You were not hired to think". (*I.M.* p. 355). When he adheres to the dictates of others, he loses his autonomy and suffers betrayals repeatedly.

Contradictory definitions given by others bewilder him. The society invents negative labels for him and expects him to live up to them. It tears him apart, and symbolically emasculates him. "When a child has no sense of how he would fit into the society around him, he is culturally deprived." (*G.T.* p. 72).

He must defend himself against the encroachments of those who would use him as a slide-projection screen for their own preconceptions. In the process his own being is blotted out; hence he is isolated and invisible even in the presence of others. In the end he becomes invisible to himself. The defect of vision resides in the beholders as a consequence of moral blindness.

He has to convince himself that he is not self-hating and defensive and that he does exist in the real world. He tries to make others feel that he exists. An array of questions clamours his attention. He asks what good it does to destroy the enemy who actually does not see him, and what he can, an invisible man do to throw off the bondage of this blindness on the part of others. He also wonders how he could be blamed if at times he acts irresponsibly and why he should assume responsibility, when the whites refuse to see him, to recognize his existence and acknowledge his service. He does not know to whom he should be responsible. He is in no mood to accept the answers that others furnish to the questions he asked. It takes him a long time to make the liberating discovery that he is no body but himself. He will no longer blind himself to the light of the truth. He would like to define himself. "When I discover who I am, I'll be free" (*I.M.* p. 185) and he also realizes "I am what I think I am". (*I.M.* p. 286). To achieve this the protagonist plunges into the depths of his life and his recollection of past experiences. His final destruction of his briefcase of printed papers, which together make up the total picture of his false selves becomes a vital act in his own liberation. He seeks the meaning of his past experience as it bears on his conception of self and the world.

People "don't solve problems of history by running away from them." (*G.T.* p. 279). Their unknown history does not stop having consequences even though they ignore them.

Each stage in the protagonist's personal history corresponds to an era in the social history of black Americans. His sojourn in the college corresponds to "Reconstruction" after the black's Emancipation in 1863. His journey towards the north represents the "Great Migration". His experience in Harlem and in the Brotherhood reflects the "Great Depression". "*Invisible Man* can be read as a symbolic history of the Negro in the U.S. during this century."[13] The protagonist assumes three major roles (a) a student at a southern black College, (b) an industrial worker in the north and (c) a political activist in Harlem. It also represents the migration of blacks from the south to the north, from the farms to the factories and from the nineteenth century to the twentieth century.

In the first section of *Invisible Man* the narrator recounts his experiences in the south. The first episode battle royal contains elements of sex, blindness, violence, money and sadism, all of which recur throughout the novel. Ellison "as a literary person trying to make up stories out of recognizable experience, and as one who was reading a lot about the myth and the function of myth and ritual in literature." (*G.T.* p. 49) saw the battle royal as a rite which could be used to show racial divisions in the society and reinforce the idea of white racial superiority.

After the battle royal, the hero gets a scholarship to the state college for blacks. Historically, this section deals with the spectre and philosophy of accommodation enunciated by Booker T. Washington, the spokesman for the blacks in the U.S. from 1895 to 1915. He aimed at placating the white south by renouncing social equality for blacks and accepting white supremacy in an attempt to pave the way for attaining an improved socio-economic status for blacks. The hero accepts Washington's dictum and aspires to a position of leadership like Washington's. He says of himself, ".... I visualized myself as a potential Booker T. Washington." (*I.M.* p. 15). It is because he accepts this philosophy that the hero is given a scholarship to the college.

When the protagonist is expelled from the college he decides to go to New York. The second section deals with the narrator's experiences as a newcomer to the urban, industrial north. The hero's journey from the college to New York has historical significance, for the trip follows the major migration pattern of blacks in America which began around 1910 and continues to the present day.

In the south the protagonist has lived in a segregated society where he knows and is always reminded of his place at all times. In the north he encounters a white society which is largely indifferent to him and which would prefer to assimilate him by destroying any cultural and racial identity he might have.

The hero's experiences at Liberty Paints also have historical significance. It is his first encounter with large industry and labour unions. Blacks were most often excluded by unions, and as a result, from gaining employment. This led black leaders to proclaim that the employer, because he provided jobs, was the blacks' best friend.

The refusal of white American throughout history to recognize the black is made evident by the presence of Lucius Brockway, who represents the blacks upon whose labour America has been built since its inception. Not only have the blacks formed part of America since its inception, but America exploited blacks for its present - day prosperity. The blacks had little acquaintance with the labour union movement and therefore they were exploited by employers in their attempts to break unions. The hero is, in fact, hired by Liberty Paints because he will not have to be paid union wages.

Since blacks were used in labour disputes, as strike breakers, the union members suspect the narrator of being a company spy and decide that he must be investigated before he can join the union - a requirement that is not necessary for white men joining the union. The narrator recognizes the racial prejudice of the other members. Ironically the prejudiced union members address the narrator as "brother." Brockway has no desire to join the union; indeed he fears that the union is trying to grab his job. Most labour unions have traditionally been racist organizations, denying membership to blacks.

As the result of an explosion, the hero is sent to the factory hospital. This section is in fact a parodic version of slavery and Emancipation in which selfhood and past are destroyed. The hero escapes from those who plan to lobotomize or castrate him. These plans symbolize the attempts of the white society to obliterate the black's cultural identity. The historical significance of this part of the novel is revealed when the doctor says of the hero's condition, "It has been developing some three hundred years ---", (*I.M.* p. 180). The hero is pronounced cured when he can remember neither his own name nor the name of his mother; he is judged fit for American society when he has been stripped of his cultural heritage.

When the hero goes north, rather than escaping from the folk culture of the south, he re-encounters it. As the result of the break with his past, the black is without cultural roots in either the black world with which he refuses to identify, or the white world which refuses to permit him to share its life.

"Because of their social isolation and lack of a cultural tradition, the members of the black bourgeoisie in the U.S. seem to be in the process of becoming no body."[14]

The hero finally articulates the discovery and acceptance of his heritage when he buys a yam and eats it on the street. It is only when he can accept his roots that he can discover his true self.

During the depression of the 1930's several black intellectuals and writers turned to the Communist party as a means of fighting racial and economic injustices. Ellison had first-hand experience with radical politics and his early writings appeared in *New Masses*, a Communist periodical. Both Wright and Ellison thought that the party gave voice and vocabulary to the blacks.

Wright analyzed the position of the blacks in a racist society and saw the Communist party as an agency of genuine improvement for the working class, both black and white.

Wright's intellectual inquisitiveness brought him into conflict with the iron discipline of the party. He began to experience the party obligations as a strain on his creative efforts. Hence he felt constrained to leave it.

Ellison on the other hand saw the party as the last and most sinister attempt by whites to manipulate the blacks. The Brotherhood in the novel is more interested in preserving and perpetuating its own civilized values than "meeting its commitment to others or even seeing those others as people."[15] This experience formed the basis for the section of *Invisible Man* that deals with the Brotherhood, a transparent version of the Communist party. Thus the novel also presents a portrayal of the black intellectuals' flirting and subsequent repulsion from the Communist party.

Ellison's commitment to the development of dynamic black leadership is reflected in all his writings.

> I was very much involved with the question of just why our Negro leadership was never able to enforce its will. Just what was there about the structure of American society that prevented Negroes from throwing up effective leaders? Thus it was no accident that the young man in my book turned out to be hungry and thirsty to prove himself that he could be an effective leader. (*G.T.* pp. 44-45).

During the protagonist's stay in her apartment, Mary Rambo talks constantly about leadership and responsibility, "You got to lead and you got to fight and move us all on up a little higher" (*I.M.* p. 196). A leader can rock the society to its very summit.

Later when the protagonist watches an eviction along with others an onlooker observes that "all they need is a leader." (*I.M.* p. 203). A mixed feeling of anger and shame finally ignites the hero's first act of leadership, his extempore speech to the crowd.

An effective organization and infrastructure are the needs of the hour to develop a potential leader. They have no money, no intelligence apparatus, and no communication network and no newspaper or any other medium. One of the reasons the Brotherhood is attractive to the hero is that it is effectively organized.

Jack says that the people always generate their leaders, but he believes that leaders are made, not born. Emma, a woman in the Brotherhood says that leaders are eventually destroyed by the people, who "chew them up and spit them out" (*I.M.* p. 230). The enabling condition of effective leadership is clearly shown to lie in self-discovery and the attainment of individuality.

Two types of leaders are seen in *Invisible Man*, the one is that of unconditional acceptance of the supremacy of whites advocated by Washington and Bledsoe, typifying the standard rags-to-riches formula and the other is the unqualified rejection of community as represented by Ras.

Bledsoe is a manipulative power-monger, a ruthlessly self-serving leader, and a statesman who carried black's problems to those above them, even unto the White House. He traces his success to his ability to feign humility. His humility is only a performance. Ras on the other hand is wrong but justified, crazy and yet coldly sane but dangerous as well. Ras is the precursor of the black power militants who struggle to survive a society in which criminals, at times, go unscathed and maniacs lead the gullible masses.

Ellison's attitude towards leadership is the third type, the positive one. But, for this attitude to prevail, the black leaders must learn the meaning of the myths and symbols which abound among the black people. The problem is self-knowledge, not of individual but of the group, that would turn a popular leader into a pragmatic and inspiring one. The protagonist comes to realize that a truer channel for his energies would be to understand and to record black experience. To record, however, is not to lead. It is an assertion of free will and call for action. But his memoir may be considered as a portrait of a young man as a potential black leader in the making.

Oratory, on street corner, in pulpit, or on rostrum remains a vital part of black culture. The protagonist identifies himself in the prologue as an orator, a rabble rouser. His talk as a child in Easter programme, his high school graduation speech, his college declamation, his impromptu anti-eviction harangue, his Brotherhood address, his funeral oration for Tod Clifton are instances of his progress towards leadership.

Throughout the funeral oration, the protagonist employs the techniques of a demagogue, keeps his audience spellbound, and restrains them from action but in the Epilogue he takes up the act of writing. Now "the act of writing commits him to action.... A writer's communication with his audience -- citizens, some of whom may also be other writers -- may be an act of leadership."[16]

Another commitment that Ellison fulfills in his writings concerns black-white sexuality and sexual stereotypes. The root cause of prejudice and discrimination is the question of pigmentation and the answer lies in accepting the inescapable integration of whites and blacks. The whole problem should be viewed in the light of miscegenation as it has been taking place in America ever since blacks landed there.

The American society is "controlled by the taboos built around the fear of the white woman and the black man getting together." (*G.T.* p. 61). The first half of *Invisible Man* contains a number of such socio-sexual references: the black woman who speaks with such ambivalent feelings about her white master-lover in the Prologue, the nude blonde dancer watched by the white men and ten black boys in the battle royal scene, Trueblood's and Norton's incestuous adventures, the prostitutes of the Golden Day and the contrast between the cartman's lusty singing about his love for his ugly, but sexually fulfilling woman and the homosexual pass made by Mr. Emerson's son who appears truly concerned about the injustice done to the protagonist by Bledsoe's letters of introduction, but desires only a homosexual relationship. Mr. Emerson's son asks the hero: "What I mean is, do you believe it possible for us, the two of us, to throw off the mask of custom and manners that insulate man from man, and converse in naked honesty and frankness?" (*I.M.* p. 141) There are equal number of references in the second half of the novel grounded in the experiences of the protagonist himself. His encounter with Emma in her posh apartment disturbed not so much by the close contact, as the sense that he had somehow been through it all before.

Probably he remembers incidents like the battle royal which reveals the motive of black male sexuality, and taboo white women, and of white rituals to effect the symbolic castration of the black male. When he overhears Emma's cynical remark about his not being black enough for the Brotherhood's purposes, his immediate response is: "I'd like to show her how black I really am." (*I.M.* p. 230) Emma asks him to dance, fulfilling the prediction of the vet on the bus going north "in New York, you might even dance with a white girl." (*I.M.* p. 117). Emma is not the only white woman to make sexual overtures to him. It is a stereotype introduced to prove the primitive sexual vitality of the black male stud and to dramatize the deleterious dimension of the dehumanizing dynamics of black-white interaction. The black has been made to function as an image of sensuality of unhampered social and sexual relationships.

Ras asks the protagonist if he has joined the white-dominated Brotherhood because they give him their stinking woman. In Ras's analysis the white man betrays and subjugates the black mainly putting white strumpets in front of him, while keeping the good white women locked up, by telling them that the black man is a rapist. Ras's analysis is brutal but frank. But such distorting and dehumanized ideas disrupt the social fabric of America.

Ellison affirms that in spite of everything, the destinies of blacks and whites in America are interwoven. Despite the presence of brutalities of racial violence, Martin Luther King Jr., in the year 1963 believed that the whites "have come to realize that their destiny is tied up with our destiny and their freedom is inextricably bound to our freedom."[17] Ellison was committed to show that such a realization was required on the part of the blacks and whites in his short story "Slick Gonna Learn"[18] published in 1939.

The black Americans are part of the whites as well as apart from them and subject to die when the whites die. The forte of the blacks and whites is "the mystery of how we are many and yet one" (*G.T.* p. 129).

Just when his pregnant wife most urgently needs a doctor's care, Slick is laid off his job at the Hopkins plant and is left with only a few dollars. Desperate for cash he finds himself in a crap game and loses his dollars and asks Bostic, a local pimp for a loan, Bostic refuses. The pimp then suggests that Slick should sell his wife to him if he wanted some money. Blind with fury, Slick attacks both Bostic and a white policeman on the scene. For striking a whiteman, Slick finds himself in court.

The firing of Slick precipitates the story's crisis. The judge releases Slick from custody in order to avoid attracting the attention of city reporters who may try to investigate the Hopkins plant layoffs. Seeing Slick released from court unpunished, the police attack Slick on his way home in the rain. Stumbling down the highway, Slick is hailed by a white truck driver who rescues Slick. Black and white worker's co-operation is dramatized in the final scene.

Slick achieves a sense of his power and worth as a human being through violence. He also learns to view his predicament not only in a racial context, but from the perspective of the working class revolution, both black and white.

When Ellison began writing his reviews he was modelling his criticism and fiction after Richard Wright's "Blueprint for Negro Writing". Wright's literary manifesto of 1937, influenced the younger writers tremendously. In his essay "Recent Negro Fiction"[19] Ellison commended Wright's collection of stories, *Uncle Tom's Children* valuable both as literature and as radical political statements.

He also hailed Wright's *Native Son* as one of the finest American novels of its time. Wright, said Ellison, exemplified the high possibilities in black life. The praise *Native Son* received in "Recent Negro Fiction" was almost its last from Ellison. In his commentaries in fifties and sixties Ellison attacked *Native Son's* realism and radicalism.

Although Ellison recognized that Wright's hero, Bigger Thomas was fighting against oppression and exploitation, he never could accept Bigger as an adequate portrait of the black Americans. Bigger failed to represent vital essences in black experience and in universal human experience. And though *Native Son* was based on the latest sociological findings and radical political perspectives, it seemed to present a narrow view of black life, a view that was not, finally, realistic and optimistic.

According to Ellison, Wright's autobiography *Black Boy* was influenced by other studies of human personality, its form is shaped by black American blues. According to Ellison,

> The blues is an impulse to keep the painful details and episodes of a brutal experience alive in one's aching consciousness, to finger its jagged grain, and to transcend it, not by the consolation of philosophy but by squeezing from it a near - tragic, near - comic lyricism. As a form, the blues is an autobiographical chronicle of personal catastrophe expressed lyrically. (*S.A.* p. 78-79).

For Ellison the lyrical ritual elements of folk jazz vindicate the truth that each individual develops his uniqueness without clashing with the neighbours and that it is "an art of individual assertion within and against the group. Each true jazz moment... springs from a contest in which each artist challenges all the rest"; and represents "a definition of his identity: as individual, as member of the collectivity and as a link in the chain of tradition". (*S.A.* p. 234). He explained that if the blues, record life's pain they also suggest the "possibility of conquering it through sheer toughness of spirit." (*S.A.* p. 94). Ellison pointed out that the environment itself is the true subject of *Black Boy*. Since Wright emphasized the power of negative forces of environment rather than the individual's ability to overcome them, Ellison came to fear that Wright was more interested in politics than in art. Ellison was committed to depict black American life in more positive light than Wright had done. He was not for the rigid outlines of the deterministic world presented by Wright. He "felt that Wright was over committed to ideology" (*S.A.* p. 16). Therefore, he opted for the magic world of possibility he found outside the bounds of literary realism.

He resented being thought of as 'the new Richard Wright,' so he pursued his artistic individuality so vigorously that at a certain stage in his career Ellison started looking for points of departure from his mentor. Ellison admitted that he was an admirer of Wright; their meeting came about through his own initiative, was encouraged by Wright to learn the technique of the literary craft and had his first piece of writing published in Wright's *New Challenge.* It was Wright who gave him a sense of direction in his writing career. But Ellison denied that his relationship to Wright was even that of a disciple.

It is true that Wright and Ellison sprang from backgrounds that were similar in certain details and different in a few others. "Wright and I were united by our connection with a past condition of servitude and divided by geography and a difference of experience based thereupon." (*G.T.* p. 199). Wright's early experiences were bitter, and he possessed the talent, unaided by any formal education. Ellison belonged to a middle class family. He was educated properly; he studied music, he knew what being a Renaissance man meant and wanted to be one of those too. He was born in the state of Oklahoma which had been a sanctuary for fugitive slaves and had attracted many of the descendants of the freed slaves. It was a territory of hope as a land of opportunity unlike the racist state of Mississippi.

Thus the backgrounds of the two men were decidedly different. "I wanted to write about American Negro experiences and I suspected that what was important, what made the difference lay in the perspective from which it was viewed" (*S.A.* p. 16).

It is this difference between the two men - a difference in their backgrounds, which led to a difference in the perspective from which each viewed black American's life-that makes their commitments, therefore their writings different. Wright wrote tragedies whereas Ellison's *Invisible Man* is a bitterly ironic, but like all tragi-comedies it has an incongruously affirmative ending.

Ellison has always evinced a keen interest in the idea of a responsible humanity. The black American desires to infer meaning from his existence for which he has been able to determine no real purpose. He is an outsider in his own country, a man trapped between the concepts called "black" and "white" world and that servility is embodied in the "black". Wright's Bigger chooses violence, crime, and vengeance as the answer to his problems.

Ellison is consciously committed to the discovering of an answer to this question as it affects the blacks. Ellison endows his protagonist with a higher level of consciousness, than that of Bigger. He comes to reject the vision of himself as a victim. Instead he assumes responsibility for his own destiny.

Protest is an element of all art, but Ellison would not limit protest to the social or political objection. The protest may be against the limitation of human life itself. The ideal of the novel is a transmutation of protest into art. Ellison does not approve the view that suffering is the only real black experience and that the true black writer must always be fuming and fretting. He points out that he belongs to "a tradition which abhors as obscene any trading on one's own anguish for gain or sympathy.... It takes fortitude to be a man and no less to be an artist" (*S.A.* p. 111). True novels must convert the cry of an anguished soul into a song of life. This is what Ellison sees as the final nature of his fiction or of any art. It includes the reconciliation possible in recognizing the humanity of those who inflict injustice. He is aware of the blackness of life and he is not plaintive about it. He has made statements deploring the dehumanizing pressures that the blacks have to put up with. But at the same time *Invisible Man* is the most powerful artistic representation of the blacks under these dehumanizing conditions. It is also a statement of the human triumph over those conditions.

According to Ellison his novel protests against the agonies of growing up. It is against the problems of a man trying to find a method in a white-dominated society to behave in a manly way. It protests against the tendency of converting art into a political weapon. It also protests against the forces of society which saps a man of his individuality and subdues his humanity. Ellison declares that if the novelist "tells the truth, if he writes eloquently and depicts believable human beings and believable human situations, then he has done more than simply protest... his task is to present the human, to make it eloquent and to provide some sense of transcendence over the given, that is, to make his protest meaningful, significant, and eloquent of human value" (*G.T.* p. 63).

The language of such novels should confront the inequalities, pessimism and self-abnegation of our society forthrightly and offer images of human fraternity, hope and self-actualization.

Ellison wanted to present the predicaments of the black Americans, without tears or complaints and to go beyond protest and struggle and to reveal the universal elements of an abiding human condition. He wanted to identify with the larger American culture despite segregation, oppression and alienation. Like America itself the black American may be described as a synthesis. His life is an attempt to reconcile certain antithetical ideas embodied in the terms: Europe and Africa and black and white. His writings assert love and possibility. His protagonist announces that the hibernation is over and a decision has been taken to leave the underground chamber to seek a socially responsible role in the world outside. The protagonist's achievement is that he has become a writer and that is the socially useful role he was looking for. The major significance of his story is his ability to tell it-to articulate and to shape into artistic form what weighed so heavily on his mind. With the telling comes a self-understanding and objectivity.

Ellison deals primarily with black experience at a time when tremendous change in black consciousness is taking place. There is a dispute over the fidelity of *Invisible Man* to the condition of blacks in America. Ellison became a prime target of attack by Marxists, black nationalists and militant black writers for his allegedly narrow, elitist view of art. These critics reject the political and cultural assumptions behind Ellison's approach and expect him to be actively involved in causes on behalf of the black community. For Ernest Kaiser, Ellison's writing is "unemotional, uncommitted, and uninvolved in his people's problems."[20] James McPherson quotes a black girl student yelling at Ellison "Your book doesn't mean anything... you are an Uncle Tom." He also quotes Leslie Fiedler's remark: "Ah, Ellison." "He is a black Jew."[21]

Black aestheticians such as Addison Gayle Jr., argue that by underlining the universality of his work and vision, Ellison avoids the specific political responsibilities of the black writer, and condemn his art as "simply a celebration of the racial acquiescence."[22]

Such views are inimical to the thrust of Ellison's writings and a simple failure to understand his moral purpose, his commitment. Ellison's hero does not deny his racial roots, he embraces all aspects of his black past by declaring "I yam what I am!" (*I.M.* p. 201). He leaves his subterranean refuge with a new vision of himself, resolved not to be cocooned in any prescriptive and restrictive social, political and cultural categories or literary conventions.

John Henrik Clarke has complained that "when Ellison's book was published, we had every expectation that his talent would extend beyond literary creation and would be given over, at least in part, to his people's struggle for survival,"[23] Ellison, by contrast has consistently maintained that to go beyond literary creation would be to distort seriously his actual commitment as a social agent. He desires to serve his society as a writer.

Ellison avers that "the major responsibility for the quality of art doesn't belong to the critic or to the public, but to the artist."[24] His social consciousness is as intense as his dedication to art. His pronouncements such as: "I wasn't and am not, primarily concerned with injustice, but with art." (*S.A.* p. 169) and "I can only ask that my fiction be judged as art; if it fails, it fails aesthetically, not because I did or did not fight some ideological battle." (*S.A.* p. 137) lead the investigation on to find out how far he has succeeded in fulfilling his artistic commitments in his writings.

§ § §

NOTES

1.   Ralph Ellison, *Going to the Territory* (New York: Random House, 1986), p. 128. Further references to this source will be abbreviated to *G.T.* and parenthesized in the text.

2.   Ralph Ellison, *Shadow and Act* (New York: Random House, 1964), p. 174. Further references to this source will be abbreviated to *S.A.* and parenthesized in the text.

3.   Ralph Ellison, *Invisible Man* (New York: The Modern Library, 1952), p. 3. Further references to this source will be abbreviated to *I.M.* and parenthesized in the text.

4.   Valerie Smith, "The Meaning of Narration in *I.M.*, in *New Essays on I.M.* ed. R. O'Meally, (New York: Cambridge University Press, 1988), p. 42.

5.   *Commentary*, 13 (June 1952), p. 608.

6.   Jacqueline Covo, *The Blinking Eye: Ralph Waldo Ellison and His American, French and Italian Critics, 1952-1971* (Metuchen, N.J.: Scarecrow Press, 1974), p. 15.

7.   Kerry McSweeney, *Invisible Man: Race and Identity* (Boston: G. K. Hall, 1988), pp. 17, 16 and 15.

8.   Irving Howe, *A World More Attractive* (New York: Horizon, 1963), pp. 112 and 114.

9.   *Saturday Review*, 24 (October 1964), p. 60.

10.   J. N. Heermance, "The Modern Negro Novel" *Negro Digest*, 13 (May 1964), pp. 66-67.

11.   "American Fiction: The Post-War Years, 1945-65" *Book Week* (26 September 1965), pp. 1-2.

12.   Richard Bjornson, "The Picaresque Identity Crisis", in *The Novel and its Changing Form* ed. R. G. Collins (Winnipeg, Canada: University of Manitoba Press, 1972), p. 16.

13.   Russell G. Fischer, "*Invisible Man* as History", *College Language Association Journal*, 17 (1974), p. 339.

14.   Franklin Frazier, *Black Bourgeoisie* (New York: Collier, 1962), p. 28.

15.   Alan Nedal, *Invisible Criticism: Ralph Ellison and the American Canon* (Iowa City: University of Iowa Press, 1988), p. 138.

16.   John F. Callahan, "Frequencies of Eloquence: The Performance and Composition of *I.M.*" in *New Essays on I.M.* ed. R. O'Meally, (New York: Cambridge University Press, 1988), p. 87.

17.   "I Have a Dream", *Black Protest Thought in the Twentieth Century* ed. August Meier (Indianapolis: The Bobbs Merrill Co., 1965), p. 349.

18.   "Slick Gonna Learn", *Direction*, 2 (September 1939), pp. 10-16.

19.   *New Masses*, 40 (5 August 1941), pp. 22-26.

20.   "A Critical Look at Ellison's Fiction", *Black World*, 20 No. 2, (December 1970), p. 57.

21.   Cited in James Alan McPherson's "Indivisible Man," in *Ralph Ellison: A Collection of Critical Essays* ed. John Hersey (Englewood Cliffs, N.J.: Prentice Hall, 1974), pp. 46 and 49.

22.   *The Way of the New World: The Black Novel in America* (Garden City, New York: Doubleday, 1975), p. 257.

23.   *Black World* (December 1970), p. 30.

24.   Ishmael Reed et. al., "The Essential Ellison" *Y'Bird Magazine*, Vol. 1 No. 1 (1977), p. 131.

CHAPTER SIX

RALPH ELLISON - PART TWO

Ellison's primary objective in writing *Invisible Man* was to create a work of art. His non-fiction also confirms the priority of art over protest that many critics have attributed to him. According to him if "the writer exists for any social good, his role is that of preserving in art those human values which can endure by confronting change." (*S.A.* p. 21). His *Invisible Man* "is not a great Negro novel; it is a work of art any contemporary writer could point to with pride."[1]

It is a portrait of the artist. As in the epics, the protagonist of the novel goes through a series of initiatory experiences from which he emerges as a new man, a human being with divine powers to create: an artist. He goes through several stages in which he acts out his conflicting sub-personalities and at last when he wins his freedom, he is reborn as the artist.

The nameless hero begins his career in a southern town as a naive adolescent who dreams of becoming educated and pleasing the white community. The narrative is the story of his expulsion from this Eden of illusion. His grandfather's "sphinx-like deathbed advice poses a riddle" (*S.A.* p. 58) and becomes a key problem for him. "I want you to overcome 'em with yeses, undermine 'em with grins, agree'em to death and destruction, let'em swoller you till they vomit or burst wide open." (*I.M.* p. 14). Each stage in his life proves that his art will be born out of blood, frenzy and humiliation. The battle royal sets the ball rolling.

At the second stage Dr. Bledsoe and the blind Barbee who says "see ahead" are pictures of "tempters." The "fall" from the college paradise occurs when the hero inadvertently shows a trustee of the college the seamier side of black life outside the utopian college ground. For this sin the punishment is fall from grace and expulsion.

The great "exodus" follows the expulsion, the protagonist's migration from the rural south to the urban north. The letter that he carries along with him is a "device": the message that the character carries contains his fate. The message is, "Keep This Nigger-Boy Running." (*I.M.* p. 26).

The paint factory is the place where the hero's unconscious act of "revolt" is staged. The act of rebellion culminates in a furnace explosion with its images of "inferno", and a loss of consciousness which functions as the ritualistic "death" of the initiate. The scene that follows in the factory hospital is clearly a strange vision of birth. The hero lies in a womb-like box. Recovering consciousness, he feels his limbs amputated; he is like an infant. The delivery is complete with the literal cutting of an umbilical cord. The old personality is dead and the hero has a new "rebirth." In order to achieve the new life of the ritual, the father must be slain. The notion of the great white father and the simple black children can be seen in terms of the relationship between father and sons. The hero's decision to know his racial heritage is equivalent to his act of rebellion. All the whites and the black baiters are seen as father-figures against whom the hero must rise against.

After the factory explosion the hero begins a new life mothered by Mary. He joins the Brotherhood. With the concept of maternity conferring new birth, all initiates become brothers. The action concludes with a vast apocalyptic image of the end of the world in the form of Harlem tumult. The hero tries to return to the mother. The running ceases only when he is driven into an underground cellar, the dark womb, while the white authority figures demand his submission and try to castrate him. The castration acts as the ultimate dispelling of illusions. Here the powers of reproduction are scarified and scattered everywhere forever renewing life. Having descended into the pit and darkness the hero has gained the right, the ability and the responsibility to prophesy.

Ellison's commitment to present the hero's search for self-discovery through the western and Christian metaphor or the inferno can further be understood by associating the battle royal with the realm of violence; the encounter between Trueblood and Norton with the realm of incontinence; Bledsoe with the realm of fraudulence; Lucius Brockway with Lucifer. Dante's mary appears as Mary Rambo, Cerberus, the three - headed dog has its counterpart in Dupre, who wearing "three hats upon his head" (*I.M.* p. 407) presides over the inferno of the Harlem riot. Ellison is also committed to the use of mythic and folkloric patterns in *Invisible Man*. The use of folklore enabled Ellison to achieve stylistic effects, provided the novel with a richness of structure and propelled its themes and images into a dream world beyond that of social realism.

Ellison's plot bears a remarkable similarity to the basic structure of the ubiquitous folktale in its basic motifs or functions. After reading Lord Raglan's *The Hero*, Ellison "noted about twenty-two aspects of character, and experiences that he attributed to most heroes." (*G.T.* p. 43). The journey in search of fortune, the supernatural knowledge of languages (the hero's oratory), the initiation rites, descent into the underworld, the substitute eye image (Brother Jack's glass eye) the trickster and magic amulet (the iron-leg link of Brother Tarp) are some of the striking folk elements found in *Invisible Man*.

The initial situation of the hero is typically folkloric, neither his parents, nor other brothers and sisters, are mentioned. The hero's story begins with a piece of advice from an elder; he is advised by his grandfather. The series of incidents which immediately follow may be taken as variations on the theme of the advice being violated. Because the hero is, naive and feckless the villain gains a crucial information about the hero. Some fraud or deception is attempted - Bledsoe dupes the hero into thinking that the letters of recommendation are really favourable. This act of villainy is done because of his lack of status, employment and economic security. The hero is sent into "Exile." He is a "victim-hero," bewitched, goes willingly to his doom. In New York he encounters several ordeals: tested for his masculinity by Emerson's son, attacked by Brockway, questioned by the doctors, spewed out onto the streets as a new man and rescued by Mary. The hero receives the "magical potion": He eats yams. He has been ignorant of his foes, uncertain of his friends, unsure of his own purpose. He discovers the object of his search, the people of his race and their culture. Because of his oratorical powers he is spotted, respected and controlled by the Brotherhood. He is pursued by his enemies. He misleads people into thinking that he is the protean Rinehart. Disappears down the hole, remains hidden for sometime for performing some feat of strength or endurance. The note of triumph is unmistakable. A "marriage" of true minds that of the author, hero, and the reader takes place. As a result of this the reader may now recognize the hero in spite of his hibernation. A "transformation from ranter to writer" (*S.A.* p. 11) takes place.

The hero's move from innocence to experience and from reticence to expression is activated by folk forms. His acceptance of black folklore and folk culture and black music keeps him sane in the riotous realm of north. Without his folk tradition, without the "shit, grit and mother wit" (*I.M.* p. 134) inherited from the past life of black Americans, he is truly a nobody, an invisible man. These folk elements affect the very structure and texture of Ellison's writings. "*Invisible Man* is a veritable compendium of folk tales, folk songs, spirituals bebop, jive (and other elements of jazz), sermons, jokes, boasts, riddles, street rap, conundrums, aphorisms, eulogies, political oratory, and the dozens."[2]

Folk tales, originated in the slave era are put to effective use by Ellison. "When I listen to a folk story I'm looking for what it conceals as well as what it states" (*G.T.* p. 289). The archetypal blackman of slave folk tale is John who comically and constantly says 'no' to his white Master and the slave system he represents. The stereotypical black man of the plantation tradition is Sambo. His speech is heavily idiomatic, his tempo slow. He grins, sings, fawns and otherwise says 'yes' to the Master. John who always outwits and outtalks his Master may appear to acquiesce, but he manages to subvert Old Master's intentions. He is the artist disguised as rogue. Sambo may appear mischievous, but he is fundamentally loyal. Ellison attempts to reconcile the two images, as though they were mirror images. The tale of pitting Brer Rabbit against Brer Bear is identified with the hero when he runs afoul of characters like Bledsoe, Brother Jack, and Brockway who constantly try to trick and trap him. Even the names of persons and characters have magical transformations. Ras's name refers to 'race'; the name has fairly obvious connections with his pan-American ideology. It echoes the ancient Ethiopian title and refers to the black belligerency of Jamaica's Ras Tafarians. The titles "Exhorter" and "Destroyer" reverse the Biblical precedent noted by the hero's grandfather, "You start Saul, and end up Paul". (*I.M.* p. 288) Saul the destroyer is transformed into Paul the Christian exhorter, but Ras moves in the opposite direction. The principal exhorter is the hero himself.

Ellison draws materials from black folk tales to convey his ideas. 'Mister Toussan' is the story about a white man Mr. Rogan, who refuses to allow Buster and Riley to eat cherries from his orchard.

The boys dream too about a flight through time and tell the tale of 'Mister Toussan' inflating the Haitian revolution of 1781 and Toussaint L'Ouverture's part in it. Buster and Riley are dubious historians of the Haitain revolt. They tell the story and convey the essence of the tale: a black hero has come forward to fight and deliver his people from white dominance. This is based on heroes battling against all odds for their people's freedom. This tale affirms the black folk values of boldness and independence; its form is based on the 'call-response' pattern in sermons, songs and stories.

Buster suggests that they sneak around the back of Rogan's house to steal some cherries. The boy's identification with Toussan moves them to action. They have a right to break away from unjust social restrictions: to assert their human rights over Rogan's property rights. The Toussan story has inspired the boys to be free even if necessary to pilfer freedom emphasizing the fact that for the blacks in America "art is a way of possessing destiny." (*G.T.* p. 32) somehow.

Black American music may not correctly be considered in isolation from main stream American music. But one cannot deny that the black Americans shaped the beat and the decorative melody at the core of the American music by imposing a heavy layer of African jungle chants and rhythms upon the European materials they found in the land of enforced adoption. For the blacks music is a balm:

> "Art thou troubled?
> Music will calm thee." (*S.A.* p. 193)

They have long utilized music to soothe their weary souls. For them God shows His face in music.

One can hear a number of minstrel melodies, folk songs, and rhymes throughout Ellison's writings. For example his book of essays *Going to the Territory* draws its title from Bessie Smith's song, "Goin' to the Nation, going to the terr'tor." In "Mister Toussan" the protagonist muses with his friend on what he would do, given wings:

> "I'd go to New York ....
> Or any where else colored is free."[3]

In the background a woman sings the spiritual, "All God's Chillun Got Wings" with its theme on freedom. In *Invisible Man* a number of moving expressions couching the traditional response of blacks to their plight such as (a) "The old longing, resigned, transcendent emotion" (b) "Lead me to a rock that is higher than I" (c) "They picked poor Robin" after the hero's meeting with Mr. Emerson's son, (d) opening bars of Beethoven's fifth symphony in the factory hospital, (e) "Jelly, Jelly, Jelly/All night long" from a juke box in a Harlem bar and (f) "There's Many a Thousand Gone" at Tod Clifton's funeral, are only a few examples.

The blues, the dominant musical form of the blacks with emphasis less on man's relation to God and more on man's anguished life on earth are also used appropriately and most tellingly. The novel begins and ends with a reference to the blues sung by Louis Armstrong namely (a) "Black and Blue" and (b) "Buddy Bolden's Blues" (c) when the narrator is expelled from the college, the sound of an "Old guitar blues plucked from an out-of-tune piano" drifts towards him, (d) in New York when the hero encounters Peter Wheatstraw who sings "Boogie Woogie Blues" to him (e) later, Mary Rambo is overheard singing a Bessie Smith, and (f) a loud speaker blares out a languid blues as the hero walks along 125th street.

The Paint factory's motto "If It's Optic White, It's the Right White" echoes the black folk rhyme:

> If you're white, you're right.
> If you're brown, step around.
> If you're black, get back![4]

Albert Murray is of the view that "*Invisible Man* was *par excellence* the literary extension of the blues."[5]

The "blues hero," according to Murray, represents qualities perfected by the blues soloist. For him "Improvisation is the ultimate human (i.e., heroic) endowment..."[6] Like the blues singer, the hero recounts his story with style, irony and a sense of absurdity viewing his grief and glory in terms of adventure and romance. Blues language and rhythms thus resound throughout *Invisible Man*. The blues provide the vehicle for coming to terms with the painful details of life. For

Trueblood conquers his fearful guilt by expressing himself in the blues. The hero finds the blues, the like of which he has heard since childhood, oddly fascinating, Peter Wheatstraw, strolling in Harlem, warns the hero not to disdain southern black folk experience in the north. Mary Rambo, Trueblood, Wheatstraw and Brother Tarp -- all these characters in the novel are sustained and strengthened with the hope by singing the blues. Bessie Smith's blues sung by Mary Rambo remind the hero of his commitment as a black-youth-of-promise, to ameliorate his people's suffering. Whenever he is despondent his hopes are rekindled by the blues songs and spirituals.

Blues singers are historians in the sense that they project lasting themes, forms and images of their culture in their songs. The hero learns from the blues of the wisdom of his forefathers, the humour, bitterness, love and the will to endure. Through the acceptance of the blues, the hero moves from shame to pride in his tradition. Like the blues, spirituals and gospel music provide a bridge to the past. Within these songs exists a celebration of the will to endure even the worst disasters. They are songs of encouragement and exultation. The blues enable him to discover that he can be free only when he accepts his own heritage.

The hero attempts to play out the roles that whites have assigned him. He finds that all those roles are different but all of them are dehumanizing like variations on a theme. He fails in all those roles. He asks himself Armstrong's punning question, "What Did I Do to be so Black and Blue" (*I.M.* p. 6). He has tried to play the game according to the rules but has each time discovered himself more battered. Thus each episode serves almost as an extended blues verse.

Since the blues, is by its very nature a record of past wrongs, pains, and defeats, it serves to define the singer as one who has suffered, and in so doing it has provided him with a history. As the novel develops, the hero takes on the role of black Everyman, whose adventures and cries of woe and laughter become the history of a people. As a high-school boy in the south he is a "Tom"--little better than a dark entertainer, in college, a Booker T. Washington, accommodationist. When he moves north, he works as a union labourer interested in Communism. Finally, he becomes a Rinehart, Ellison's word for the drifting, alienated, urban black who sells dreams and fantasies indiscriminately to all the people.

Sermons play an important part in *Invisible Man.* In the Prologue, the hero hears a black preacher sermonizing on "The Blackness of Blackness." (p. 7). A few characters adopt the styles of black preachers. Homer A. Barbee claps his hands and chants in sermonic style. The hero's first speech at the Brotherhood rings with spirited repetition of the sermon. He depends on shouted responses from the audience as a black preacher does.

Black humour is at once a means of catharsis and a form of "Code communication" to laugh at the foibles of others and to laugh at oneself. Wit, reflexive irony, sarcasm and pun have been corpus of ethnic jokes, songs, and folk tales for centuries. During slavery times, comic tales formed a mythology for a largely illiterate and scattered captives and fugitives. They provided a relief from pains and a cementing force for the blacks. While their experience was unrelieved agony, their escape from it was through the materials of comedy. Humour, in its simplest and direct forms pervaded black culture, permeated secular music from field shouts to party songs. All the forms of black music reveal sharp wit, self-edification and veiled criticism.

Ellison has used all the resources of folk humour: black slang and black vernacular. People crack jokes to tell the truth and truth is the funniest of all jokes. *Invisible Man* is not strictly a satire, but Ellison creates satiric effects through irony. *Invisible Man* relates the adventures of an innocent mind through a maze of deceptive appearances moving from comfortable naivete to desperate experience. It relies on hyperbole and equivocation to create a symbolism for vanity and deceit. Ellison generalizes his irony to encompass a whole culture and its history. The view point is consistently that of the victim aimed at showing the drawbacks of the white society and their effects on blacks. "Verbal comedy was a way of confronting social ambiguity" (*G.T.* p. 138).

Folk humour is used as a metaphorical description of black life. The native folk tales, folk ways and folk heroes are regarded as the embodiments of survival in the hostile world. These enable the blacks to cleverly outsmart their adversaries and to manage not only to survive but to win. So they welcome any play on words or nuance or gesture which give expression to their secret sense of the way things really are. The game of "Playing the dozens" is a slanging match based on witticisms about the enemies' ancestry and legitimacy and signifying or verbally outscoring an adversary. Patterns of survival take the form of games or verbal duels which require insight and ingenuity on the part of the people. From slanging matches to bawdy jokes come the revelations of the effect of white rape-physical and spiritual-of the black people.

A fund of satirical material comes from objects of everybody life-objects of scorn which blacks associate either with oppression or with capitulation. Eating of yams, the solutions of skin whitening, the hair straightening combs, the curling iron, the lucky stone, the knocking bones, life insurance policies stamped "Void," etc., are the objects which reveal the facts of self-loathing forced on the black mind by a white world oriented toward social status and material comforts. The Sambo puppet which Clifton peddles is a sign of white manipulation of blacks and also symbolizes the hero, dancing on Brother Jack's string.

Satiric caricatures of Tuskegee Institute, its founder Washington, Bledsoe, Norton and Rinehart are monstrous images in the nightmare of the hero. Through them Ellison portrays the betrayal of black cause from the inside - Washington's ideal of humility is shown as a compound of obsequiousness and machiavellian plotting. The whites in the battle royal are cartooned as utterly degenerate; sexually deprived, and inebriate. Norton and Emerson are liberal but through their liberalism they are shown as dissemblers. Lucius Brockway presents the image of the slave who works to keep white society running. Political radicalism of Brother Jack and the Brotherhood are revealed as hollow and deceptive.

The invisibility metaphor which controls the ideas of the novel is extended to include the invisibility of the fences and fortifications of white America exhibiting the gross discrepancy between what seems to be and what is, and what is and what ought to be.

Satire is traditionally a kind of minority report and Ellison depicts reality through caricature, fantasy and hyperbole to show the feelings behind the facts of black existence and uses them for comic effect to bring home salient features of the absurdities of American life. Ellison uses simple invective as a satiric tool, his ironic points are made subtly. His anger and humour are articulated through the magic of words to unveil hidden truths. Language, at times conceals the truth that experience should convey. This blending of ironic exposure and scrutiny in the end commit us to decide whether this tragic force to continue to play itself out or whether we should act swift so that the forces of love and understanding can triumph in the long run.

In factual prose, ambivalence of meaning is a fault to be condemned, but in Ellison's writings it is condoned and treated as a prized asset since intellectual challenge is sparked by ambivalence. "I too have become acquainted with ambivalence." (*I.M.* p. 81).

The protagonist's grandfather offers an ambivalent advice. The obvious meaning might appear to be that blacks can best survive in a white society by pretending to accept the values of whites, by giving verbal assent to the majority will. These signs of acquiescence are intended to do more than guarantee black survival. It adumbrates a strategy designed to destroy the white enemy. It is a double - edged tool serving the cause of black survival and white destruction. The blacks are urged to undermine the oppressive society by pretending to uphold it. But at the same time, one must be wary because by pretending to agree one may, indeed, agree.

The American society stands for the idea of democracy and freedom. The blacks see in their daily lives that these values are abrogated by whites and those blacks who have felt that their own destiny lay in complying with power rather than principles. It means a license to exploit and treat with condescension one part of the society by the others. It also means the idea of "oneness" of the society, the necessity of a single destiny for a people bound by the same societal bonds. After the recital of his high-school graduation speech and his participation in the battle royal with his blindfolded companions the hero dreams his grandfather is with him at a circus and commands him to open an official envelope in his briefcase. He wonders whether this dream is simply a forewarning of what he must escape or it is a predication that such pressure by society is necessary to generate in him sufficient insight to finally overcome the limitations of race.

He once again dreams of being pursued by his antagonists to make him conform to their ways, and who having failed to achieve their purposes, castrate him, announcing that they are freeing him of his illusions. He asks himself whether the price of true vision is the surrender of one's manhood and whether he could actually become free only when his pursuers realized that he was free. He wants to know whether he could be visible only if his fellowmen choose to acknowledge his visibility.

Ellison is committed to show that a man's worth depends more on his own positive action than it does on the negative action of others. The hero realizes that "Irresponsibility is part of my invisibility" (*I.M.* p. 11).

Ellison insists that the hero is entirely responsible for all of the circumstances that lead him to his misfortunes. But one can ask why the hero refuses to assert and achieve his own humanity. It is because the nature of the racist society prevents it. Ellison is attacked by a few for not putting enough punch in his attack against racist society. It is difficult to understand how one can say that an unmasking of the evils of an oppressive society is not an attack on that society. If one is really committed, he exposes evil in order to correct it. On the basis of such logic, *Invisible Man* is truly an attack upon racist society.

The novel traces one young black man's search for self-discovery in a white-dominated world, which has warped his self-image and moulded his values to its benefit and to his disadvantage. The hero takes various avenues to truth, and finds to his dismay that each way leads back to the same old lie.

Invisible Man explains in the Prologue the need for deciding a sense of one's self and of one's relationship to a world which is not one's self. Such a sense seldom comes by the passage of years.

Invisibility is a positive recognition of a selfhood different from that which is established by society. The hero knows what he is not. He is not any of the roles society expects him to play. But yet he does not yet know what he is.

Writing is action, and as the hero writes out his search he begins to discover his lost self. "And the act of writing, for all its admitted ironies, becomes a part of that resistance and an expression of the commitment to others, to society, which the protagonist now professes. The book is itself a public gesture, and its publication stands as evidence of the hero's reemergence into the world and his belief in the efficacy of communication."[7]

Ellison is committed to the deliberate exploitation of language and the "skillful exercise of the sheerly rhetorical elements - the flash and filigree - of the artist's craft" (*G.T.* p. 7) as a device of artistic communication. The hero's rhetorical skills earn him recognition as an orator and organizer. The social and intellectual values, the political tactics and the propaganda techniques adopted by the Brotherhood stresses the significance of rhetorical methods. The hero realizes that the possibility of securing leadership means "climbing a mountain of words." (*I.M.* p. 288). He believes that there was magic in spoken words and he turns out to be a speech - maker.

The hero's graduation speech is really a recital of Washington's "Atlanta Exposition". The hero talks "automatically" with his mouth bloody from the battle royal. The mechanical delivery and the dry diction project a view point that is unreal and culturally barren. The realities that have been obscured by Washington's ideology are symbolized by the hero's bloody saliva, the electrified rug, and the battle royal itself.

The oratorical traditions of the college have been conceived as a satiric imitation of Booker T. Washington's ideas and rhetoric. The Founder is a Washingtonian archetype who depended on his gift as a moving orator. The Washingtonian ethic has deprived the black peasant of his cultural roots and the substitute offered by the Founder is racial humility.

The veteran's anonymity is a satiric parody of the nameless Founder. The apparent confusion of his style is really a methodical process that undermines the precise formality of blind Barbee's logical appeals. The Veteran's warning to Norton about the other veterans that "They might suddenly realize that you are what you are..." (*I.M.* p. 71) embodies a deliberate disorder of his delivery and it is very mechanical. Both the contrived disorder of the vet's delivery and the palpable chaos at the Golden Day are combined as natural forms of self-expression which offset the precise formality of college rhetoric and the unreal artificiality of Bledsoe's "flower-studded waste land". (*I.M.* p. 29).

It has been recognized that Norton's personality is integrated with Trueblood's incestuous experience. Trueblood's crime is the projection of Norton's subconsciously incestuous memories of his daughter. A comparison of the subconscious memories of Norton and Trueblood's unpolished directness of his narration of his adventure contrasts ironically with more inhibited, but equally undeniable desires. The self-conscious deception of Norton's artificial disguise is exposed to the realities represented by Trueblood's act and by his unlettered style. Norton's good intentions disguise racist assumptions and Trueblood's self-reliance and his mesmerizing story - telling ability are inseparable elements.

Trueblood's dream is not limited to the incest theme, it also projects another social taboo, miscegenation, which ironically extends Norton's rhetoric revealing his interest in the destiny of blacks in the south to a logical conclusion.

The political rhetoric of the Brotherhood is just as symbolic as the style of Barbee or Norton. The black moderate, the white liberal and the Communists use language to project their scientific approach. As power-mongers they use rationalism to manipulate human beings like robots. The Brotherhood's hostile reaction to the hero's first speech is adjudged to have been "incorrect" that is wordy, hysterical, politically irresponsible and dangerous because it was the antithesis of the scientific approach. The repressive figure of Supercargo in the Golden Day links the formalities of southern oratory to the "scientific approach" of the Brotherhood. Ellison is committed to expose the empty "correctness" of the Brotherhood's ideology. Bledsoe's college is shaken by the tipsy veteran's brawl at the Golden Day. The bloody consequences of Trueblood's incest contribute to the undermining of Norton's idealistic pretensions. Washington's doctrine of black progress through - humility is countered by the racist violence of the battle royal. And the mechanical manipulations of the Brotherhood are opposed by the eloquent vitality of Ras's violent exhortations. Ras uses rhetoric self-consciously; his exhortations are self-expressive.

Accustomed as he is to the restraints of Washingtonian humility, the hero is awed by Ras's impudence. Ras ridicules the sham of the Brotherhood's science by pointing to its manipulative purpose. Ras's analysis reminds the hero of an earlier betrayal - the horror of the battle royal. The glib oratory of college leaders and the Brotherhood's scientific terminology are both opposed to the rough energy of Ras's rhetoric.

Ras sees his style as the expression of suppressed cultural instincts. He uses such exhortation as an emotional catalyst for self-recognition and cultural integrity. The energy of his rhetoric aroused cultural and emotional awareness. His rustic eloquence effectively challenges and exposes the empty refinement of the Brotherhood's hollow principles.

When the hero addresses the Harlem mob, he realizes that the mob is angry, but he urges them to be wise. Thereafter, he becomes more self-expressive, and in the process, more explosive. He discards the restraint in favour of uninhibited self-expression and social conscience. The exhortation which is born out of his cultural awakening is opposed to the inane rhetoric of social responsibility. It also contrasts with the scientific jargon that the Brotherhood applies to the identical situation.

His eulogy to Clifton lacks superficial links with the party's political aims or terminology. His initial determination to use scientific rhetoric for political purposes is transcended by the human experience that informs the old mourner's blues. Emotional experience rather than the political issues dominates his funeral oration. And once again, unbridled self-expression displaces the cliches of ornate speech. Hence his oration infuses new life into the concept of Brotherhood.

He discards all formal rhetoric during his last confrontation with Ras. Even as he tries to placate the Destroyer, eloquence fails him. He knows that it is futile since he has no words and no eloquence.

The hero's grandfather is the archetype of the ideal exhorter. Thus, when the hero, finally realizes the meaning of the old man's style the hero is ready to emerge from his hole. And he returns as an effective exhorter, for his story is a communicative process between the narrator and the reader. Writing shapes and communicates his commitments to his society and to art.

The symbols in *Invisible Man* are not something artificially implanted; they are not alien elements incongruously imposed. They are convincing and they indicate the depth of Ellison's commitment to artistic sensibility, the richness of his talents and the range and power of his vision. They form an integral part of his creative and communicative process. A "work of art is, after all, an act of faith in our ability to communicate symbolically." (*G.T.* p. 15).

In *Invisible Man* a number of objects are given symbolic significance through which commonplace materials are forced to undergo a creative metamorphosis. For example (a) Yam signifies blacks cultural root in the south, which the hero had been denying; it indicates his willingness to savour both the things he enjoys and the memories they conjure up. (b) when Tarp says that the piece of field steel he is giving the hero has "a heap of signifying wrapped up in it," (*I.M.* p. 293) he means that this reminds him of his years as a slave and a reminder of the oppression of the blacks in America. When Tarp gives the link to the hero, he is performing a symbolic act of the passing the torch variety. (c) Barbee, who falls flat on the chapel platform after finishing his speech, mythologizing the life of the college founder, is as blind as his namesake, the Greek epic poet (d) the eruption of Jack's previously unmentioned glass eye on to the table after a heated exchange at the Brotherhood meeting (*I.M.* p. 358) relates to the theme of sight and insight, seeing and not seeing through Barbee's blindness and Jack's half-blindness, (e) the subtle and suggestive symbolic effects of the scene in the paint factory in which the hero is told to mix ten drops of black paint into buckets of white paint have layers of meaning and (f) Clifton's Sambo puppets symbolize the black members of the Brotherhood who are manipulated and victimized by the white leadership.

The nameless blackman of the short story "King of the Bingo Game"[8] lashes out against the restrictive and stultifying aspects of the victimized life style of the blacks. He needs money to defray the medical expenses of his wife. In order to win the jackpot, the bingo wheel must stop between the double zero. The wheel becomes the interpreter of his destiny. Realizing the meaninglessness of his life, he deliriously revolts against his fate. His unwillingness to stop turning the bingo wheel shows his intention to subvert the game. He knows that as long as he presses the button, he can control the jackpot. But when the card is finally extricated, the wheel ironically registers between the double zero. He finds that he is not allowed to win the jackpot or the game. Ellison employs the game to depict life as a risk and a gamble and the powerlessness of blacks in America.

A Cadillac stands for wealth, social climbing and prestige. Dr. Bledsoe is admired as an influential leader of his people as he also happens to be "the possessor of not one, but two Cadillacs." (*I.M.* p. 78).

Eight portions of Ellison's second novel highlighting the adventures of Reverend Hickman, and his adopted son Bliss, who disappears into the white community passing for white later surfaces, as a senator from a New England State with a new name Sunraider have been published. In "Cadillac Flambe"[9] Ellison deals with a bizarre incident of the burning of a Cadillac and its political and ritualistic significance. A black jazz musician, Lee Willie Minifees hears Sunraider on the radio ridiculing blacks, especially those who own Cadillacs. Minifees who owns a Cadillac drives his white car on to the Senator's lawn and sets fire to it and makes a speech denouncing the Senator's contempt for the blacks. The immolation by Minifees is an extreme gesture springing from the frustration of having no adequate means of replying or making himself heard above the majestic roar of the

Senator. Minifees is not a politician but he fights for respect and freedom. His action symbolizes the burning of American greed, materialism and vanity. He brings home the truth that Americans are "given to eating, regurgitating, and also, re-eating" (*G.T.* p. 19) even their most sacred words; they do not live up to their lofty national principles and that the divorce between promises and practice most involves the black Americans. In rejecting Cadillac he rejects American idolatry of machines. He also celebrates human solidarity over mechanical efficiency. The Cadillac is the symbol of decadent display. He would rather walk, crawl or fly than drive a Cadillac. His act also shows that political hypocrisy of men like Sunraider will go up in smoke.

His act is also a ritual drama. He imitates all the ceremonial activities of the soldiers, salutes the car, douses the car with petrol and fires a flaming arrow at it. He makes a speech, sings, "God Bless America" and holds his wrists to be handcuffed.

Ritually too, the burning is an act of participation, an offering to God imploring Him to lift an old curse and to allow a new birth. The Phoenix and Icarus myths are remembered. The incident takes place during the spring and so it heralds the spring in black American lives.

Minifees is a free bird but Sunraider's words ground him. The use of fire and bird symbols bring to the mind Phoenix and the rituals of birth, death and resurrection. The rite is one of fertility and celebration.

The act of Minifees is one of political daring and protest. It is a plea for justice and a cry for man's redemption. It is also a symbol, a hope that a new life will be born once again.

Twentieth century American fiction especially realist and naturalist fiction was inadequate to delineate the diversity of American life generally, and had shown itself irresponsible in portraying the realities of black life. Ellison required the penetrating imagination that allowed him to look beneath the surface and to interpret the manners and motives of the society that enslaved, excluded and exploited the blacks.

Ellison employs a variety of narrative styles in *Invisible Man.* In the south where the hero's sense of certainty had not yet been challenged, a more naturalistic treatment is given; in the north where he feels a loss of certainty in the flux of life in a megapolis, the expressionistic style is employed. After the hero's expulsion from the Brotherhood the surrealistic style is used. In the last portion of the novel during the Harlem carnage where the hero "experiences nothingness as the existential condition of being alive"[10] the existential mode is adopted.

The problem of perception is exemplified by the symbol of blindness or a defective vision or a failure of perception. The physical depriva- tion of sight suggests the difficulty of achieving genuine vision. Perhaps we are able to see only that which we are prepared to see. Thus the hero has a white blindfold placed over his eyes, when he rehearses the speech on the virtues of humility. The statue of the Founder is frozen in a gesture of either loosening or perhaps binding more securely - the veil that obscures the vision of a kneeling slave. Norton queries the incestuous Trueblood about the "need to cast out the offending eye" (*I.M.* p. 40).

Homer A. Barbee who advocates the principles of the Founder as the black's enlightenment and freedom is shown to be blind at the end of his speech. When Emerson allows the hero to see the contents of Bledsoe's cruel letter, he cautions the hero: "There is no point in blinding yourself to the truth." (*I.M.* p. 146).

The metaphor of physically impeded vision is used to reflect the theme of blindness. For example the narrator delivers his first speech for the Brotherhood in an arena where a boxer had lost his sight in the ring and had died afterwards in a home for the blind.

Brother Jack's glass eye falls out in the heat of an angry discussion. The visual implications at times turn rather on a new way of seeing than on the deprivation of sight. The narrator talks about the veil of appearances being torn away. At the eviction scene he begins to alter his vision to a truer sense of the past.

The futility of paper identities like his high-school diploma, the scholarship and the letters of recommendation given by Bledsoe indicates the illusion and reality of such papers.

The animal imagery graphically highlights Ellison's theme that when one human being treats another as an object or animal both are dehumanized or become bestial considering that "Aesop and Uncle Remus have taught us that comedy is a disguised form of philosophical instruction; and especially when it allows us to glimpse the animal instincts operating beneath the surface of our civilized affectations." (*G.T.* p. 146). The hero's grandfather advises his son to live with his head "in the lion's mouth" (*I.M.* p. 13). The lion is the white man, "The men roared" (*I.M.* p. 22) as the hero in the battle royal struggled for the coins on the electric rug.

Because the white men treat the black boys as animals and the naked white woman as a sexual object, ironically the white men reduce themselves to animals. The men sink their "beefy fingers" (*I.M.* p. 17) into her flesh and run "howling after her" (*I.M.* p. 17). The boys are called "sonsabitches" (*I.M.* p. 18) and "cautious crabs" (*I.M.* p. 19) by the men. Later, the hero lunges for a coin on the rug and the electricity shakes him "like a wet rat" (*I.M.* p. 22) and when thrown onto the rug, his muscles, twitching "Like the flesh of the horse stung by many flies" (*I.M.* p. 22). The naked white lady too, is described as a "fair bird girl" (*I.M.* p. 16). At the end, the hero is given a "calfskin briefcase" (*I.M.* p. 25). The boxing ring and the electrified rug in the battle royal symbolize their socially confined existence and the perils involved.

The white men treat the blacks and the white lady not only as animals but also as inanimate objects. She is like a "kewpie doll" (*I.M.* p. 16) wearing an abstract mask. The hero compares himself to inanimate objects: a "ginger cookie" (*I.M.* p. 18), a "foot ball" and a "dish-rag" (*I.M.* p. 23).

Ellison sees the racial situation in battle royal as a circus. The hero calls Tatlock a "stupid clown" (*I.M.* p. 20) and the boy thrown onto the rug looks like "a wet circus seal" (*I.M.* p. 22). At the end, the hero dreams that he is at a circus where his grandfather "refused to laugh at the clowns" (*I.M.* p. 26). The clowns represent black men who put on an artificial smile to mask their humiliation and get what they want.

"America is a land of masking jokers." (*S.A.* p. 55) so references to clowns appear throughout the novel. "Jokers" give the hero in the prologue the reefer which produces the hallucination. When the furnace in the paint factory explodes and the hero lies in a state of traumatic amnesia he feels like a clown. He has to realize that the white establishment is the enemy, and it furthers its own ends, treating the blacks like clowns.

The use of colour-pairs such as black-white, blue-gray and gold-brass highlight the racial problem. The "lily-white men" (*I.M.* p. 20) smoke "black cigars" (*I.M.* p. 15). The attendants wear "white jackets" (*I.M.* p. 21) and the briefcase is "wrapped in white tissue paper" (*I.M.* p. 25). The black boys are "blindfolded with broad bands of white cloth" (*I.M.* p. 17).

Later in the novel at the paint factory the hero must mix ten drops of black chemical into a cream-coloured base to make white paint, a symbol suggesting that racial colour is most noticeable when contrasted. The hero is sent off to a black college with a briefcase bought from "Shed Whitmore's shop" (*I.M.* p. 25) whose name rearranged reads shades more white; that is, whites are a shade whiter when there is educational segregation. The hero's dilemma is that he is neither black nor white, but "ginger-colored" (*I.M.* p. 18).

The gold-brass dichotomy foreshadows Ellison's commitment to reveal the disparity between illusion and reality and the contrast between the black's expectations and other's intentions. Because of his skin colour he thinks he is visible, but in fact he is invisible. He spends his energy scrambling for gold coins that are just brass tokens. In his dream he reads a message contained in an envelope a short message in letters of gold which spell out a brazen reality of their being kept running. The hero proves himself to be immature because he graduates from "Greenwood High School." (*I.M.* p. 23). The colour red stands for hatred or anger. When the boys fight, the men have howling red faces. In describing the effect of his knockout the hero says, "The room went red as I fell" (*I.M.* p. 21). The men watch, with red faces swollen from anger and laughter, as the boys scramble on the electric rug.

Suppressed by the predominantly white society around him, the black American is often held back even by members of his own race. He may even feel a sense of despair, despondency, vague guilt and an urge toward violence. Ellison chooses to present his hero's search for definition in part through the western as well as Afro-American tradition. Ellison declared: "I have no desire to write propaganda" (*S.A.* p. 17). So he does not limit himself to the black literary tradition. In fact, he deplores the black writer who comes along and tries to write on the models of other black writers rather than the best writer regardless of race, class: "Too often we've been in such haste to express our anger and our pain as to allow the single tree of race to obscure our view of the magic forest of art." (*G.T.* p. 278). He also does not believe in limiting himself to the American literary tradition for he knows that the blacks are a continuation of a European civilization. As a result, Ellison overcomes the restrictions of mere protest literature; he escapes the charge of provincialism by striving towards universality. He admires Faulkner, even though he was a white southerner since he felt more deeply about the blacks than most black writers. He wanted to achieve the same kind of freedom as a black writer and as a man.

Ellison drew inspiration from a host of literary luminaries as well as from the religious scriptures and folk tradition. He points out that while one can do nothing about choosing one's relatives, one can, as artist, choose one's ancestors. Wright was, in this sense a "relative," and Hemingway an "ancestor". He goes a step further and asserts that Hemingway "was in many ways the true father" (*S.A.* p. 141). Ellison is committed to prove that racial kinship is not a matter of choice; literary influence is.

A critical study of T. S. Eliot's *The Waste Land* was a beginning of Ellison's literary education and it was the beginning of his change from a would-be trumpeter into a writer. Ellison uses folklore in his work not because he is a black, "but because writers like Eliot and Joyce made me conscious of the literary value of my folk inheritance. My cultural background, like that of most Americans, is dual ..." (*S.A.* p. 58).

Ellison shares a sustained relationship with Emerson. Ellison's middle name is Waldo. Emerson's dictum that "A man must ride alternately on the horses of his private and public nature, as the equestrians in the circus throw themselves, nimbly from horse to horse"[11] inspired Ellison to lay the foundation of his art built on the simultaneous assertion of individual and the conception of a socially committed self.

Ellison referred to his novel as "the portrait of the artist as a rabble-rouser." (*S.A.* p. 17). This links Ellison with Joyce, Both *Invisible Man* and *The Portrait of an Artist as a Young Man* exhibit the search for self-discovery and discovery of their vocation as artists and writers.

He admits that he learns from Hemingway his sentence structure and how to organize a story. Ellison's early writings bore the definite influence of Hemingway.

Homer Barbee's speech about the Founder rephrases Whitman's elegy for Abraham Lincoln, "When Lilacs Last in the Dooryard Bloomed." Ellison employs Whitman's symbols such as lilac, star and thrush for entirely opposite reasons than did Whitman to refer to the racial betrayal brought about after the emancipation of slaves. Whitman's optimism and his faith in democracy are called into question when his symbols are employed to the Founder, whose successor Bledsoe is shown as a veteran of manipulative powers.

The narrator of *Invisible Man* goes to great lengths to declare his affinity by locating himself in the great American tradition of tinkers: "That makes me kin to Ford, Edison and Franklin." (*I.M.* p. 6).

Richard Wright's short story "The Man Who Lived Underground" and Dostoevsky's *Notes from Underground* provided Ellison with the idea of modern underground man and Ellison blended it with the metaphysical topics of the underworld and inferno taking clues from classical literature.

The success of Ellison as an artist depends on his commitment to transcend the form and achievement of his literary ancestors and relatives and to create something new, something rich with his own art.

Though Ellison did not write *Invisible Man* as a comparison or a counterpart to H. G. Wells' *The Invisible Man* is bound to have more in common with Ellison's novel than just two words of the title, assuming that Ellison chose his title deliberately. Ellison committed himself to give the subject invisibility more depth, meaning, and significance. Wells's aimed at showing the perils of power without proper control and the development of the intelligence at the expense of human compassion and commitment.

The hero of H. G. Wells's fiction, Griffin's predicament is his self-induced invisibility whereas the invisibility that is associated with blackness and its effects such as isolation, discrimination and persecution is imposed by others. When Griffin is attracted towards that strange idea of invisibility he works "like a nigger"[12] for its realization. Probably Wells used the comparison that Griffin is working like a nigger without being aware of the significance of his tale, that is the connection between blackness - as a racial concept and invisibility.

Wells's invisible man is a social misfit, who sees invisibility as a solution to his problem. Once he achieves invisibility he becomes a problem as an object of curiosity and horror. For Ellison invisibility is a problem arising from his racial heritage for which he needs a solution.

Griffin has plans of all the wild and wonderful things he has now impunity to do. His power is to be used for his own advantage and against his fellowmen. But Ellison's hero sees the possibilities of his invisibility.

Griffin robs his father, and he proves himself to be a potential danger to the society as he is devoid of human feelings. He is killed at the end and so ends the story of the odd and evil experiment of H. G. Wells' invisible man. Ellison's hero too is considered a possible threat to the established order. But he has no nefarious designs against this order. He reveals the injustice, the sickness inherent in that order which gives him the moral right to overthrow that order. The existing order is depicted as morally deviant since it usurps his inalienable rights and tries to subjugate him. Wells pits the individual against society, whereas Ellison emphasizes the individual's commitment within the moral law to reconstruct his society.

It is true that Wright triggered Ellison's literary career. But Ellison does not approve the idea that he was *influenced* by Wright. Though Ellison was artistically depended upon Wright, later in his career he got artistic emancipation from Wright, "I respected Wright's work and I knew him, but that is not to say that he 'influenced' me as significantly as you assume" (*S.A.* p. 139-40) and declared "No, Wright was no spiritual father of mine." (*S.A.* p. 117).

Wright's story "The Man Who Lived Underground" is widely thought of as a parallel to and a source of *Invisible Man*. The parallels are that both central figures are blacks, and that both are driven underground, and are committed to their social responsibilities.

Ellison once admired Wright for his having "converted the black's impulse toward self-annihilation and 'going underground' into a will to confront the world, to evaluate his experience honestly and to throw his findings unashamedly into the guilty conscience of America". (*S.A.* p. 94).

The metaphor of the underground, to Wright is a sewer, a receptacle of waste, whereas to Ellison it is a "coal cellar, a source of heat, light, power and through association with the character's motivation, self-perception." (*S.A.* p. 57). For Wright's hero it is the time for retrospection whereas for Ellison's protagonist it is the time for introspection. For both of them the underground is the realm of perception, the realm which reveals the truth of their lives. Both protagonists are being pursued, hunted, and driven underground. There they recognize the guilt of those who drive them and also realize their own commitments.

Both of them cogitate about the role of religion in black's life. It is a criticism of black religious commitments that promises redemption without human brotherhood. Prayers alone cannot prevent exploitation and blot out injustice without a commitment to practise what is being preached.

Wright describes how the underground man hides in a coal-bin while a white man carries shovels of coal to a nearby furnace. Apparently Wright suggests that the white man drains the resources of power without recognizing the black's humanity. In Ellison's novel the power or coal is not being drained either by whites or blacks. This reminds the readers of the Biblical parable of the buried talents. Ellison's hero is committed to the use of his innate talents and latent potentialities. While Wright condemns the exploitation of the blacks, Ellison highlights the refusal of America to let the blacks take part in the weal and woe of America.

Both the heroes tap power lines to furnish their selves with light and music. The implications are that America by forcing some of its people underground, is depleting part of its potential, its resources, its power. By denying blacks their due on the one hand and exploiting them on the other America fails in its commitment and becomes weaker culturally, economically, and morally.

Having accomplished the Promethean feat of stealing fire or light, both heroes employ the power to operate some music-making device, while Wright's hero connecting a stolen radio set, simply hears music, the Invisible Man, on the other hand owner of a radio-phonograph would like to hear five recordings of Louis Armstrong. He uses the stolen power to play the blues. Through this Ellison shows how committed his hero is to his racial heritage.

Wright's hero uses the stolen power to shed light upon his surroundings, while Invisible Man to shed upon himself. Wright's hero will be an iconoclast when he emerges from his hibernation while Ellison's hero will be a committed humanist and optimist. Wright's hero, when he emerges to share his vision, finds that words fail him. He is shot down in cold blood, whereas Ellison is committed to the rebirth of an artist with eloquence, vision and creativity. His artistic creation is his book.

André Malraux's books *Man's Fate* and *The Days of Wrath* inspired and influenced Ellison to a large extent. Ellison is very frank in accepting the fact that he was influenced by writers like Malraux when he says that "Books are written out of other books just as battle plans are made out of earlier strategies and tactics."[13] That is why Ellison advises the apprentice writers to read everything because one learns from the achievements of other writers but at the same time the artist's creative impulse involves a will to go beyond his forerunners and not to follow them slavishly. So the writer must choose his literary ancestors. He must avoid aping the masters. He must assimilate them and develop his own style. The artist imposes order on the world, the very process of creation; it is he who gives pattern and hence meaning to experience. Malraux opines that "every masterpiece, implicitly or openly, tells of a human victory over the blind force of destiny.... All art is a revolt against man's fate."[14]

Wright appreciated Malraux as a politically committed novelist and as a novelist who could strike a balance between his art and his message. Malraux has been described as "a man deeply committed to politics-engagé in his own language."[15]

Malraux's reflections on the psychology of arts, the creative process and his works influenced Ellison's writings, his attitudes and commitments to life and literature. That is why Ellison agrees that protest is an element of all art, though it does not necessarily take the form of speaking for a political or social ideology. But at the same time Ellison declares; "Now mind. I recognize no dichotomy between art and protest." (*S.A.* p. 169).

A novel should transcend its immediate background and speak eloquently for people everywhere. Ellison as a committed artist writes so truthfully about his own people and their problems and aspirations that he speaks eloquently to all people and speaks for all people. He declared: "I committed myself to the art and form of the novel and the discovery and articulation of the most exalted values." (*S.A.* p. 165).

Ellison has expressed the predicament of the black Americans without violating his passionate dedication to art as an agency for confronting and revealing that which has been hidden "by our cultivated incapacity to perceive the truth." (*G.T.* p. 229). This achievement throws ample light on the success of Ellison as a writer and artist with commitment.

§ § §

NOTES

1.   Harvey C. Webster, "Inside a Dark Shell," *Saturday Review*, XXXV (12 April 1952), pp. 22-23.

2.   *Dictionary of Literary Biography*, Vol. 76, p. 48.

3.   Ralph Ellison, "Mister Toussan," *New Masses*, 41 (4 November 1941), pp. 19-20.

4.   Robert O'Meally, "Introduction" *New Essays on Invisible Man* (New York: Cambridge University Press, 1988), p. 11.

5.   *The Omni-Americans* (New York: Outerbridge, 1970), p. 167.

6.   *The Hero and the Blues*, (Columbia: University of Missouri Press, 1973), p. 107.

7.   C. W. E. Bigsby, *Second Black Renaissance* (1980), p. 98.

174   R. Jothiprakash

8.   Ralph Ellison, "King of the Bingo Game," *Tomorrow* (November 1944), pp. 29-33.

9.   Ralph Ellison, "Cadillac Flambe," *American Review* (February 1973), pp. 249-269.

10.   Lucio P. Ruotolo, *Six Existential Heroes: The Politics of Faith* (Cambridge, Mass.: Harvard University Press, 1973), p. 94.

11.   Quoted in Harold Kaplan, *Democratic Humanism* (Chicago: University of Chicago Press, 1972), p. viii.

12.   *The Invisible Man* (New York: Bantam, 1970), p. 79.

13.   David L. Carson, "Ralph Ellison: Twenty Years After," *Studies in American Fiction*, No. 1 (1973), p. 8.

14.   André Malraux, *The Voices of Silence* (St Albans, Herts.: Paladin, 1974), p. 639.

15.   David Wilkinson, *Malraux* (Cambridge, Mass.: Harvard University Press, 1967), p. 1.

CHAPTER SEVEN

SUMMING UP

As authors, James Baldwin and Ralph Ellison were as essentially unlike each other as two contemporaries sharing a common situation can ever be.

The writer is in a situation and in a milieu, signifying the synthesis of all the forces which influence and illuminate the period in which he lives. The great temptation of the writer is to write for immortality and not just for his times. If the purpose of writing is to change the world, the writer must be at pains to discover and work within his unique historical situation. He should engage the predicaments and choices offered by his situation. He must participate, through his writings in the socio-political and moral struggles of his times and promote freedom and fair deal for all the dispossessed people throughout the world.

Both Baldwin and Ellison were committed to work for the removal of racial evils in American society, but at the same time their writings manifested universal outlook and therefore attained everlasting appeal. "Good art commands attention of itself whatever the writer's politics or point of view" (*S.A.* p. 137).

Baldwin changed himself from a pulpit orator to a prolific writer while Ellison turned from the trumpet to the typewriter. Even though Baldwin and Ellison drew inspiration from Richard Wright, both of them later turned out to be his bitter critics. It was their commitments which compelled them to have differing viewpoints from their idol.

Critics like Irving Howe[1] censured Baldwin and Ellison of forsaking the mission of a black writer, which constituted according to Howe an expression of anger and militant assertion of black freedom. Howe cited Wright as the most emphatic voice of black freedom in fiction and praised Wright for his predilection for protest literature. He was unhappy with Baldwin and Ellison, for their failure to carry the banner of protest as done by Wright.

Both Baldwin and Ellison resented the attempts of literary critics to rigidly restrict their role based on their race and colour. Wright saw black life blank and bitter whereas Baldwin and Ellison saw it with positive vision and hope. Their vision of black life was different from that of Wright as their commitments and sensibilities were different from those of Wright's. They were passionately committed to their own personal vision.

They were committed to the idea of human versatility and possibility which broke through the artificial barriers created to impede their advancement in American society. They refused to be trapped in the trammels of stereotyped roles.

There is a tension in their writing between the concept of geography as fate and the concept of human volition as destiny. Neither geography nor tint of skin defines the nature of life and aspirations. One's fate is determined by what one does and what one does not do. A society's destiny depends, irrefutably, upon the courage and commitment of the individuals who constitute it. The facts of geography or race are accepted as raw materials which individuals assimilate and alter by an assertion of their unique personality and will. Even as they were being conditioned by their circumstances, they knew how to soar beyond and to take what they required from the life around them and leave their footprints on the sands of eternity. They were not mere products of their socio-political predicaments. They were the shining models of humanity that could overcome inherited or imposed impediments. Literature for them provided an outlet for thwarted self-expression. They conceived of the human situation as a kind of cosmic exile and committed themselves to counter isolation

with fraternity.   They were also committed to leave the uneasy
sanctuary of race and colour to take their chances in the world of art.

The differences in the life of Wright, Baldwin and Ellison attest to the
wide spectrum of life for blacks in America. Wright, the product of
the deep south of a lower class family, and of broken home, never
forgot the misery that was his lot. He felt deeply the hurt of black
living. Hunger and violence were his family heirlooms. He was
deprived of the possibility of what he might become. Defined and
manipulated by the white south he was robbed of a sense of self-worth
and a sense of poise and direction in life. The more his society
conspired against his human dignity, the more committed he was to
assert himself. His commitment to write was born of an intense desire
to affirm his own reality. Southern blacks were forced to suit even
their speech habits to the expectations of the whites. He was cogni-
zant of the fact that to attempt to write seriously was to involve
oneself into one of the most self-destructive and almost self-murder-
ous careers.

In such a situation Wright committed himself not to be intimidated
into silence. He was determined to speak out at all costs and to
express his own self in writing. His entire life was an assertion of self
in a society in which individual perceptions of self were pitted against
its prejudices.

On the other hand, like Johnny, Baldwin was the product of Harlem
ghetto. He was the victim of penury, physical ugliness, step-father's
hatred and white racism. He was exposed to hurt and tormented by
the way he was treated. Pain nourished his courage. It was by pain
that he defined himself. He was committed to give real poetic depth
to his pain and to the polemics of black pride. He was convinced that
one must experience other people's suffering in order to experience
one's own. One must be baptized in suffering as a precondition for
love to triumph. By immersing in suffering one accepts the commitment inherent in unselfish love. "Sorrow is the only key to joy."[2]

And Ellison hailed from a lower middle class family, not in Mississippi but in Oklahoma. He felt and accepted the challenge of his background. He stepped outside his black experience and viewed it objectively. He found himself neither in the structured life in deep south nor in the apparently free and deceptively luminous nightmare life of New York.

The openness of his frontier town freed him of the kind of restrictions Wright and Baldwin experienced. Ellison grew up with the actual experience of possibilities which convinced him of the validity of personal will and effort and the viability of American democracy.

Wright's protagonist Bigger is the product of a criminal society and Wright was convinced that such a society must be changed in order to prevent the creation of more Biggers. Bigger has no other option but to kill in order to save himself. He becomes a representative actor who performs a crucial act so that others will not have to commit similar atrocities.

Unlike Wright, Baldwin and Ellison indicate an intense determination to embrace their blackness as a high value and as a means for changing the fate of America. Being black is a mark of distinction for them. For the other blacks rage and violence, religion and drugs and at times exile or suicide provide escape routes from the drudgeries of life. But for these writers their writings were the instruments for denying the attempts to mould their nature to the black stereotypes, for preserving a sense of their own selves.

Social problems are never solved by enforcing the law of revenge. Baldwin and Ellison show that anger and violence are not necessarily the only posture for an authentic black man. They share Wright's concern for the need for justice. But Wright could not shed his memories of a bleak childhood and a suffocating adulthood. Violence of Bigger or the exile of Fishbelly in his novel *The Long Dream* is the answer that Wright offered. Wright himself opted for a self-imposed exile and died as an expatriate in Paris. But Baldwin and Ellison found that America is the only arena in which a black person can hope to achieve freedom in spite of present day problems.

Baldwin was not destroyed in his attempt to withstand the violent and corrupt forces. He learned to endure and was even tempered by them. He did not believe in wanton destruction, mindless violence and motiveless malignity. He saw the church often lagging in its commitment for social justice. His hero Johnny is not converted to the church, but to the whole life of his people. The redemption that he finds is not through the grace of God, but through an affirmation of his own self.

The blacks in America have sunk so low that they have the satisfaction that they can go only upwards. Orpheus in the European legend descended into the interior self in order to find his lost Eurydice. Ellison's hero is a subterranean Orpheus who is ascending to the surface to find his own self.

The protagonists of Wright and Ellison have found themselves at the bottom. Baldwin also declared, "In a way, the Negro tells us where the bottom is: because he is there" (*N.K.M.N.* p. 111). So he must ascend.

The artist is cast in their writings in the role of a committed revolutionary fighting for radical social changes. They are "practically and magically involved in collective efforts to trigger real social change."[3] Both were committed to respond to the demands of a changing society - a society where tradition is vying with charge - and directed the change itself.

Both Baldwin and Ellison had faith in the inevitability and reality of human progress, the centrality of the individual, and the need for personal fulfillment with a tacit acceptance of personal responsibility for one's society. They also recognized the need for free thinking, for the individual to hold conflicting points of view without ceasing to function. For them the individual is shaped as a result of the collision with a public world which is simultaneously a threat and a source of opportunities and challenges.

Just as the larva breaks through all that curbs its growth and meta-morphoses into a butterfly, the individual has to fight against everything that obstructs his development and rise to his full stature. Every black who "seeks to escape from his rut or corner by vanishing, and so becomes an accomplice in his own elimination."[4]

Survival is both the secret and paramount obsession of contemporary man. If existence is an endless obstacle race for survival then the experiences of the protagonists of Baldwin and Ellison may be thought of as public documents on survival. Baldwin started his career as a writer as a means to sheer survival. Like Malcolm X. Baldwin also learned how "to view everyday living as survival"[5] Ellison's *Invisible Man* too is about the art of survival. Only the fittest can survive. But the survivals of the heroes of Baldwin and Ellison are secured with dignity in the midst of evil, terror, exploita-tion and pain. They were committed to individual freedom and social justice not through hatred and separation, not out of pity, not at the cost of self-respect but through persuasion and love. They aimed at social harmony through reconciliation since the drive towards reconciliation and unity provides "a new sense of life's possibilities." (*N.K.M.N.* p. 23).

As writers committed to the black folk tradition Baldwin and Ellison saw the blues as a tool of survival and used the folk music and art as such in their writings.

Baldwin and Ellison believed in the concept of "the surgeon's idea of pain"[6] embodying the inevitability of inflicting temporary pain for effecting permanent cure.

Wright was convinced that the whites would never give black folks a chance to lead a decent life and that the American Dream was nothing but a nightmare for the blacks. To be black was to be an outsider and outcast and so the mission of that outsider was terrorism. He was forced to inch his way toward a great blasting moment of supreme destruction. The blacks found themselves as devocalized dogs; no amount of barking released them from their dehumanized conditions. He lost faith in the healing power of love. So he was committed *to be hard.* Violence, rage and homicidal malevolence inspired his heroes and they believed that these alone ensured them manhood.

Baldwin was a spokesman and so he believed in the power of words. He wanted to seek a direct entry into the world for the sake of redeeming it from the brutality and the indecencies and to serve a truly human and humane purpose. So he was committed *to be heard.* He is remembered for his words of which he was a master and a wizard. In his words, "we comprehend the ultimate intelligence of our enforced commitment to finally bring humanity to the world."[7]

He said things that the downtrodden people longed to say. He said them right out loud, for all the world to hear. Thus he became the voice of the inarticulate masses. He preached, prayed, persuaded and proclaimed that the dooms day would be arriving soon if *status quo* prevailed. The titles of his books, reveal his passion for telling others: *Go Tell It on the Mountain, Tell Me How Long the Train's Been Gone,* and *If Beale Street Could Talk.*

Since men use words to conceal the chaos that seethes beneath the surface, Ellison did not believe in shouting hoarse. He realized that "if the word has the potency to revive and make us free, it has also the power to blind, imprison and destroy." (*S.A.* p. 24). He did not endorse the use of violence; nor did he believe in mere persuasion. For violence begets violence and a flow of words is no proof of wisdom. So he was committed *to be seen,* to reveal the unseen and to expose the gap between apparent and actual realities and promises and practices. His protagonist achieves visibility when he learns to look beneath the surface and to look for what lies behind the face of things.

Wright's protagonist is a rebel who chooses to go wrong in his own way rather then go right in somebody else's. He is a *mercenary* who embodies physical hunger and *the rifle* is his symbol.

Baldwin's protagonist is a spokesman and a witness who at times talks blasphemy, but talks his own blasphemy. He is a *missionary*, passionately introspective who embodies emotional hunger and *the Bible* is his symbol.

Ellison's protagonist is a trickster who considers it "better to live out his own absurdity than to die for that of others" (*I.M.* p. 422). He is a clairvoyant *visionary* with insatiable artistic hunger carrying a *bugle* as his symbol.

Wright's view of the world, born out of his bitter personal experiences was madly unjust and pointlessly brutal. Baldwin and Ellison attacked the plausibility of Bigger as an accurate representation of a real black person. Bigger is not only a stereotype that distorts black life into a horror story, but a reinforcement of ideas held by whites about the prejudicial criminal proclivities of blacks. Bigger is the stereotypical black man that existed in the minds of white Americans. Whites had created such stereotypes and used them as a justification for their ill treatment of blacks. Baldwin and Ellison were against such stereotypes and caricatures. They were given to optimism and insisted upon both the gloom and glory of American life. Both of them advocated individual initiative and the case for diversity. They were committed to the establishment of a society that makes room for as many individual life styles as there are individuals to create them; a society in which blacks like any other people, can create their destiny through acts of will.

Wright at times engaged in fantasies of revenge against whites for casting him out and treating him as dirt. Yet the basic commitment of his art was constantly moving toward the theme of black and white unity. For example, Wright says, "I am black and I have seen black hands raised in fists of revolt, side by side, with the white fists of white workers."[8] and "The differences between black folk and white folk are not blood or color and the ties that bind us are deeper than those that separate us...."[9]

Baldwin's writing is not just a docile appeal but a warning of an impending revolution. The choice is clear: co-existence or no existence. He told the whites: "not that I drive you out or that you drive me out, but that we learn to live together."[10]

He exhorts the whites to summon the courage to face their reality and to work toward a revolution together. He does not accept the view that hatred of whites is the inevitable result of the experience of being black in America. He does not endorse the view that hatred is the only reaction to oppression. Hatred always destroys both the perpetrator and the victim. This recognition has given rise to Baldwin's vision of the redemptive role of the blacks. In abandoning, Christianity, Baldwin never rejected the possibilities offered by the transforming power of love. He is committed to the power of love in human affairs and a sustaining influence and an abiding faith in the interpretation of the world without prescriptions of how to change. His intention was to describe the racial situation so thoroughly that the readers could no longer evade it. Baldwin is compelling the whites as well as blacks to remove prejudices from their minds and realize that the ship of America will sail with black and whites together or sink.

According to Ellison most American whites are culturally part black American without even realizing it. "Whatever else the true American is, he is also, somehow, black." (G.T. p. 111). He was committed, therefore, to explore the mystery which haunts American experience and that is the mystery of how they are "many and yet one." He is convinced that it is not even possible to isolate a black American tradition that exists independently of the other traditions which help shape the American character. He insists that the blacks are not African people, but Americans of eclectic cultural traditions and mixed bloodlines whose history and destiny are indigenous. This amply proves that the fundamental dynamics and commitment of their art is constantly moving toward the black - white unity. All Americans, irrespective of their physical features share a common past and their destinies are inextricably intertwined. Baldwin says that the black American is "the world's first genuine black Westerner." (*The Price* p. 553) and he is the cultural bridge connecting Africa and the western world. Ellison's hero also asserts the same view when he declares, "we are Americans, all of us, whether black or white." (*I.M.* p. 363).

Baldwin and Ellison are thus committed to an identity that is not black, nor is it African - it is American. The significance of Alex Haley titling his book *Roots: The Saga of an American Family* should be seen in this context. Haley has used the epithet *American* judiciously since his book has set many whites "thinking about their own families and where they came from."[11] With the exception of Red Indians all Americans have a place in the African continent to go back to. This vindicates the commitments of Baldwin and Ellison.

Both these writers exposed with equal vigour the shortcomings of the blacks as they did the weaknesses of the whites.

"The first people to do Negroes damage are usually other Negroes." (*S.A.* p. 71). Baldwin and Ellison condemned the ill treatment of blacks by whites. They also condemned the ill treatment of the blacks by other blacks. The blacks are "as a basket of crabs, wherein should one attempt to climb out, the others immediately pull him back." (*S.A.* p. 91). They deplored petty-mindedness and selfishness wherever such qualities existed.

Neither Baldwin nor Ellison was obsessed with any political creed or sociological ideology. They were, in their earlier days, closely associated with and deeply involved in the affairs of the Communist Party. But they were disenchanted with it later. The journals of the party provided a forum for their social action and indeed they had their baptism in the world of letters on the planks of the Communist press. Like their mentor Wright, they flirted with Communism for a short period and then kept themselves aloof from it. The Communists have not forgiven them for their desertion.

Richard Wright in his autobiography *Black Boy*[12] mentions a number of authors who influenced his writings. Similarly, in their essays, Baldwin and Ellison have acknowledged their indebtedness to these masters and added a few more writers like Dickens, James Joyce, Henry James, Hemingway and Emerson as writers who shaped their techniques and vision. Baldwin and Ellison have also enumerated a host of black American and African authors and artists as the source of their inspiration. The Bible, slave memoirs and other material representing their oral tradition, folk tales, myths, the blues, the jazz, the spirituals and other forms of black culture also had their indelible mark on their writings.

The writings of Baldwin and Ellison, in turn have become a source of unfailing spur and sway to the writers of succeeding generation. Toni Morrison, Larry Neal, Amiri Baraka, Alice Walker, Ishmael Reed, Al Young, James Alan McPherson, John Wright, Albert Murray and Leon Forrest are but a few writers who have appreciated the inspiration and example provided by Baldwin and Ellison on their literary career and commitments.

There are critics both black and white who dogmatically assert that literature produced by black Americans is writing by blacks solely for blacks. The term 'negritude' as defined by Leopold Senghor as "the sum total of the value of the civilization of the African world"[13] and by Sartre in "Black Orpheus" as "blackmen ... addressing themselves to black men about black men"[14] does not hold good to the black American writers as they no longer consider themselves, for historical reasons purely Africans. They identify themselves as hybrids of Africa and America and their literature is inseparable from the African and western literary traditions. Further what Sartre says about black writing in general as "actually a hymn by everyone for everyone",[15] is best applicable to the writings of Baldwin and Ellison, since they seek "to communicate a vision of experiences..." that "achieves its universality." (*G.T.* p. 242). They thought of themselves not so much as blacks or even as Americans but as human persons. They stepped out into the universal from the narrow limits imposed by their skin colour and racial realities.

"The whole American reality is based on the necessity of keeping black people out of it."[16] The impact of race upon personality is very important for Baldwin and Ellison and the pain of being black in a white dominated society moves them to literary expression. They are committed themselves to articulate persuasively and artistically the various nuances of hurt and also to the eradication of racial injustice and social inequalities. The evaluation of their writings should be done in terms of what they made of their pain and hurt artistically.

Both Baldwin and Ellison have been called "Uncle Toms." Some critics have deplored them by stating that they shirk their responsibilities as black victims and that they are too sanguine about the possibilities of human freedom in America. To an ordinary black American there "is a bitter irony in the picture of his country championing freedom in foreign lands and failing to ensure that freedom to twenty million of its own."[17] Both Baldwin and Ellison were aware of the incongruities and absurdities of American democracy. But their aim was not the destruction of the world. They intended to revamp the society and to have continuity side by side with systematic structural changes with abiding faith in the American dream, in the future of mankind and in the human capacity for renewal. They have, from their experiences, captured in their writings those forms that characterize racial situation in America and the lessons that are to be drawn by the posterity. Especially have they delineated the changes in black consciousness contributing to the evolution of a new and just social order.

In their writings one can see the signs of a turning point in black art and culture. There is now a greater freedom in the way the blacks regard themselves.

A number of things that gave Baldwin and Ellison great cause for grave concern in America have changed. The conscience of white America and as a consequence some of the aspects of American legality have changed. There is integration everywhere. Buses and public conveniences are no longer segregated. Black Senators, Mayors and other elected officials dot the land. A black American, Senator Dilman, President *pro tempore* of the Senate becoming the President of the U.S.A., after the death of the President, Vice-President and the Speaker of the House of Representatives may no longer be just an adventitious occurrence in a novel.[18] Rev. Jesse Jackson, just missed the chance of being nominated to the race for Presidentship of the U.S.A. by the Democratic Party in 1988. The day a black American becoming the President of the U.S.A. is not remote.

The commitments and the concerted efforts of Baldwin and Ellison and their writings have contributed a great deal to usher in those changes.

Baldwin's views may seem a closed book with nothing more to be expected from him, but investigations into them should go on. On the other hand, Ralph Ellison continues to write, and therefore continues to grow. *Invisible Man* still remains the sole indicator of his artistic significance. He has confessed: "I am a writer who writes slowly" (*G.T.* p. 308). He has been hibernating too long. The publication of his long-awaited second novel "will be an event, of course, but in one respect at least, it will not be a surprise. We can be certain that Ellison will not have changed his mind."[19]

Further studies on how the emphasis of Baldwin and Ellison on the autonomy of black American culture and its inseparability is endorsed or spurned by the writers who have come after them may be undertaken.

Both Baldwin and Ellison called attention to the absurdities at work within American society. Investigations may be undertaken how they have influenced the other writers in their efforts to do away with such abnormalities in American life.

Studies may be undertaken on their efforts to discover and rebuild black folklore, oral tradition, black music, and their inevitable interaction with the rest of American culture and how the writers of succeeding decades have exploited these resources and enriched American literature.

Baldwin and Ellison were committed to the idea that black American experience is a synthesis of African and western experience but it is nonetheless a universal experience. Investigations to show how far this idea has been assimilated or rejected by writers, both black and white and if so, why, may be of great significance.

A study on the impact of the writings of these two writers on the themes and techniques of the succeeding generation of writers will go a long way in vindicating the success and fulfillment of the commitments of Baldwin and Ellison, the two towering personalities in the field of American literature.

§ § §

1.   Irving Howe, "Black Boys and Native Sons", *A World More Attractive* (New York: Horizon Press, 1963), pp. 98-122.

2.   James Baldwin, *Just Above My Head* (New York: Dial Press, 1978), p. 569.

3.   Clarence Major, "Introduction", *The New Black Poetry* (New York: International Publishers, 1969), p. 12.

4.   Roger Rosenblatt, *Black Fiction* (Cambridge, Mass.: Harvard University Press, 1974), p. 185.

5.   James Baldwin, *The Autobiography of Malcolm X* (New York: Grove Press, 1966), p. 90.

6.   W. H. Auden, "Prologue," in *The Faber Book of Modern Verse* ed. Michael Roberts (London: Faber and Faber, 1982), p. 258.

7.   Amiri Baraka, "We Carry Him as US", *The New York Times Book Review* (20 December 1987), pp. 27-29.

8.   Richard Wright, "I Have Seen Black Hands", *New Masses*, 26 (June 1934) p. 163.

9.   Richard Wright, *Twelve Million Black Voices* (New York: Viking, 1941), pp. 146-47.

10.   Eckman op. cit., p. 247.

11.   Alex Haley, "Haley's Talk, Write, Unite," *Time*, 14 (February 1977), p. 72.

12.   Richard Wright, *Black Boy: A Record of Childhood and Youth* (New York: Harper and Brothers, 1945), p. 218.

13.   Cited in Willfried F. Feuser, "Wole Soyinka: The Problem of Authenticity", *The Literary Half Yearly*, Vol. XXVIII, No. 2, July 1987, p. 205.

14.   Quoted by C. W. E. Bigsby, *The Black American Writer*, Vol, I (Deland, Florida: Everett/Edwards Inc., 1969), p. 25.

15.   Ibid.

16.   James Baldwin, "Baldwin Interview", *Essence* (March 1988), p. 117.

17.   Martin Luther King Jr., *Why We Can't Wait* (New York: Harper and Row Publishers, 1963), p. 9.

18.   Irving Wallace, *The Man* (New York: Bantam Books, 1974).

19.   Louis Menand, "Liberated By Literature," *The American Review*, No. 2 (1987), p. 70.

SELECTED BIBLIOGRAPHY

1. Works by James Baldwin (listed chronologically)

(a) Books

Go Tell It on the Mountain. New York: Knopf, 1953.

Notes of a Native Son. Boston: Beacon Press, 1955.

Giovanni's Room. New York: Dial Press, 1956.

Nobody Knows My Name: More Notes of a Native Son. New York: Dial Press, 1961.

Another Country. New York: Dial Press, 1962.

The Fire Next Time. New York: Dial Press, 1963.

Blues for Mister Charlie. New York: Dial Press, 1964.

Nothing Personal (with photographs by Richard Avedon). New York: Atheneum, 1964.

Going to Meet the Man. New York: Dial Press, 1965.

The Amen Corner. New York: Dial Press, 1968.

Tell Me How Long The Train's Been Gone. New York: Dial Press, 1968.

A Rap on Race (with Margaret Mead). Philadelphia: Lippincott, 1971.

No Name in the Street. New York: Dial Press, 1972.

One day When I was Lost: A Scenario Based on Alex Haley's 'The Autobiography of Malcolm X'. London: Michael Joseph, 1972.

A Dialogue (with Nikki Giovanni). Philadelphia: Lippincott, 1973.

If Beale Street Could Talk. New York: Dial Press, 1974.

The Devil Finds Work. New York: Dial Press, 1976.

Little Man, Little Man: A Story of Childhood. New York: Dial Press, 1976.

Just Above My Head. New York: Dial Press, 1979.

Jimmy's Blues: Selected Poems. London: Michael Joseph, 1983.

The Evidence of Things Not Seen. New York: Holt, Rinehart and Winston, 1985.

The Price of the Ticket: Collected Nonfiction, 1948-1985. New York: St. Martin's/Marek, 1985.

(b) Periodicals

"Maxim Gorki as Artist." *Nation,* 12 April 1947.

"History as Nightmare." *New Leader,* 25 October 1947.

"The Harlem Ghetto: Winter 1948." *Commentary,* February 1948.

"Lockridge: The American Myth." *New Leader,* 10 April 1948.

"Previous Condition." *Commentary,* October 1948.

"Journey to Atlanta." *New Leader,* 9 October 1948.

"Everybody's Protest Novel." *Zero,* Spring 1949.

"The Negro in Paris." *Reporter,* 6 June 1950.

"Many Thousands Gone." *Partisan Review,* November - December 1951.

"Stranger in the Village." *Harper's,* 1953.

"Paris Letter: A Question of Identity." *Partisan Review,* July - August 1954.

"Equal in Paris." *Commentary,* March 1955.

"The Crusade of Imagination." *Nation,* 7 July 1956.

"Sonny's Blues." *Partisan Review,* Summer 1957.

"The Discovery of What It Means to Be an American." *New York Times Book Review,* 25 January 1959.

"They Can't Turn Back." *Mademoiselle,* August 1960.

"The Dangerous Road Before Martin Luther King." *Harper's,* February 1961.

"The Survival of Richard Wright." *Reporter,* 16 march 1961.

"On the Negro Actor." *The Urbanite,* April 1961.

"The New Lost Generation." *Esquire,* July 1961.

"An Interview." *WMFT Perspective.* December 1961.

"As much Truth as One can Bear." *New York Times Book Review,* 14 January 1962.

"The Artist's Struggle for Identity." *Liberation,* March 1963.

"A Talk to Teachers." *Saturday Review,* 21 December 1963.

"The Uses of the Blues." *Playboy,* January 1964.

"The Creative Dilemma." *Saturday Review,* 8 February 1964.

"What Price Freedom." *Freedomways,* 2 August 1964.

"The American Dream and the American Negro." *New York Times Magazine,* 11 July 1965.

"To Whom It May Concern: A Report from Occupied Territory." *Nation,* 11 July 1966.

"God's Country." *New York Review of Books,* 23 March 1967.

"The Nigger We Invent." *Integrated Education,* March-April 1968.

"Sidney Poitier." *Look,* 23 July 1968.

"White Racism or World Community." *Ecumenical Review,* October 1968.

"Sweet Lorraine." *Esquire,* 12 November 1969.

"Dear Sister..." *Manchester Guardian,* 12 December 1970.

"How One Black Man Came to Be an American." *New York Times,* 26 September 1976.

"An Open Letter to Mr. Carter." *New York Times,* 23 January 1977.

"If Black English Isn't a Language, Then Tell Me What Is?" *New York Times,* 29 July 1979.

"Of the Sorrow Songs: The Cross of Redemption." *New Edinburgh Review,* Autumn 1979.

"Notes on the House of Bondage." *Nation,* 1 November 1980.

"The Evidence of Things Not Seen." *Playboy,* December 1981.

"On Being 'White' and Other Lies." *Essence,* April 1984.

"Freaks and the American Ideal of Manhood." *Playboy,* January 1985.

"Letter to the Bishop." *New Statesman,* 23 August 1985.

2. Works by Ralph Ellison (listed chronologically)

(a) Books

Invisible Man. New York: Random House, 1952.

Shadow and Act. New York: Random House, 1964.

Going to the Territory. New York: Random House, 1986.

(b) Periodicals

"Creative and Cultural Lag." *New Challenge,* Fall 1937.

"Practical Mystic." *New Masses,* 16 August 1938.

"Slick Gonna Learn." *Direction,* September 1939.

"Ruling-class Southerner." *New Masses,* 5 December 1939.

"The Birthmark." *New Masses,* 2 July 1940.

"Afternoon." *American Writing,* ed. Otto Storm et al. Prairie City, Illinois: J. A. Decker, 1940.

"Richard Wright and Recent Negro Fiction." *Direction,* Summer 1941.

"Mister Toussan." *New Masses,* 4 November 1941.

"That I Had the Wings." *Common Ground,* Summer 1943.

"In a Strange Country." *Tomorrow,* July 1944.

"King of the Bingo Game." *Tomorrow,* November 1944.

"Flying Home." *Cross Section,* ed. Edwin Seaver. New York: L. B. Fischer, 1944.

"Richard Wright's Blues." *Antioch Review,* Summer, 1945.

"Did You Ever Dream Lucky?" *New World Writing,* 5 April 1954.

"February." *Saturday Review,* 1 January 1955.

"A Coupla Scalped Indians." *New World Writing,* 1956.

"And Hickman Arrives." *Noble Savage,* 1960.

"The Roof, the Steeple and the People." *Quarterly Review of Literature,* 10 (1960).

"Out of the Hospital and Under the Bar." *Soon One Morning,* ed. Herbert Hill. New York: Knopf, 1963.

"It Always Breaks Out." *Partisan Review,* Spring 1963.

"The Blues." *New York Review of Books,* 6 February 1964.

"On Becoming a Writer." *Commentary,* October 1964.

"Juneteenth." *Quarterly Review of Literature,* 14 (1965).

"Night Talk." *Quarterly Review of Literature,* 16 (1969).

"A Song of Innocence." *Iowa Review,* February 1973.

"The Alain Locke Symposium." *Harvard Advocate,* Spring 1974.

"Backwacking: A Plea to the Senator." *Massachusetts Review,* Autumn 1977.

3. Selected critical works by others.

(a) Books

Alexander, Charlotte A. *Baldwin's 'Go Tell It on the Mountain', 'Another Country', and Other Works: A Critical Commentary.* New York: Monarch Press, 1968.

Auden, W. H. "Prologue". *The Faber Book of Modern Verse* ed. Michael Roberts. London: Faber and Faber, 1982.

Baker, Houston A., Jr. *Long Black Song: Essays in Black American Literature and Culture,,* Charlottesville: The University Press of Virginia, 1972.

Balmforth, Ramsden. *The Problem Play and Its Influence on Modern Life and Thought.* London: Allen and Unwin, 1928.

Baumbach, Jonathan. "Nightmare of a Native Son." *The Landscape of Nightmare.* New York: New York University Press, 1965.

Bentley, Eric. *The Playwright as Thinker: A Study of Drama in Modern Times.* New York: Harcourt, Brace and World, 1982.

Bigsby, C. W. E. *Confrontation and Commitment: A Study of Contemporary American Drama, 1959-1966.* London: MacGibbon & Kee, 1967.

-----. *The Black American Writer,* Vol. 1 and 2 Deland, Florida: Everett/Edwards Inc., 1969.

-----. *The Second Black Renaissance: Essays in Black Literature.* West Port, Conn.: Greenwood Press, 1980.

Bjornson, Richard. "The Picaresque Identity Crisis." *The Novel and Its Changing Form* ed. R. G. Collins. Winnipeg, Canada: University of Manitoba Press, 1972.

Bone, Robert A. *The Negro Novel in America.* New Haven: Yale University Press, 1958.

Brawley, Benjamin. *Early Negro American Writers.* New York: Dover, 1970.

Brooks, Cleanth. "Irony as a Principle of Structure. *Literary Opinion in America,* ed. Morton Dauwenzabel. New York: Harper and Bros., 1951.

Brown, Sterling. *Negro Poetry and Drama and the Negro in American Fiction.* New York: Atheneum, 1969.

Butcher, Margaret J. *The Negro in American Culture.* New York: Knopf, 1956.

Campbell, James. *Talking at the Gates.* New York: Viking, 1991.

Caxton's Encyclopedia, Vol. IV.

Chapman, Abraham, ed. *Black Voices.* New York: New American Library, 1968.

Clark, Kenneth. "James Baldwin Talks with Kenneth Clark." *The Negro Protest.* Boston: Beacon Press, 1963.

Contemporary Literary Criticism, Vol. 42 and Vol. 50.

Covo, Jacqueline. *The Blinking Eye: Ralph Waldo Ellison and His American, French, German and Italian Critics, 1952-1971.* Metuchen, N.J.: Scarecrow Press, 1974.

Coyle, Martin. *Encyclopedia of Literature and Criticism.* London: Routledge, 1991.

Crossman, Richard. ed. *The God that Failed.* New York: Harper and Row, 1949.

Crozier, Alice C. *The Novels of Harriet Beecher Stowe.* New York: Oxford University Press, 1969.

Cuddon, J. A. *A Dictionary of Literary Terms.* London: Andre Deutch Ltd., 1977.

Davis, Arthur P. *From the Dark Tower: Afro-American Writers, 1900-1960.* Washington, D.C.: Howard University, 1974.

Davis, C. T. *Black is the Color of the Cosmos: Essays on Afro-American Literature and Culture 1942-1981.* New York: Garland Publishers, 1982.

Dictionary of Literary Biography, Vol. 76.

Dietze, Von R. F. *The Genesis of an Artist.* Nurenberg: Verbag Hans Carl, 1982.

DuBois, W. E. B. *The Souls of the Black Folk.* Chicago: A.C. McClurg and Co., 1903.

Eckman, Fern Marja. *The Furious Passage of James Baldwin.* New York: M. Evans & Company, 1966.

Eliade, Mircea. ed. *The Encyclopedia of Religion,* Vol. 2. New York: Macmillan Publishing Co., 1987.

Eliot, George. Review of *Dred: A Tale of the Great Dismal Swamp* by H. B. Stowe in *Critical Essays on H. B. Stowe,* ed. Elizabeth Ammons. Boston: G. K. Hall, 1980.

Fielder, Leslie. *The Inadvertant Epic: From 'Uncle Tom's Cabin' to 'Roots'.* New York: Simon and Schuster, 1979.

Fowler, Roger. *A Dictionary of Modern Critical Terms.* London: Routledge and Kegan Paul, 1973.

Frazier, Franklin. *Black Bourgeoisie.* New York: Collier, 1962.

Furnas, U. C. *Goodbye to Uncle Tom.* New York: William Sloane, 1956.

Gayle, Addison, Jr. ed. *The Black Aesthetic.* Garden City, New York: Doubleday, 1971.

-----. *The Way of the New World: The Black Novel in America.* Garden City, New York: Doubleday, 1975.

Gibson, Donald B. *Five Black Writers: Essays on Wright, Ellison, Baldwin, Hughes, and LeRoi Jones.* New York: New York University Press, 1970.

Gross, Seymour L., and John E. H. eds. *Images of the Negro in American Literature.* Chicago: University of Chicago Press, 1966.

Haley, Alex. *Roots.* New York: Dell Publishing Co., 1977.

Handy, W. C. *Blues: An Anthology.* New York: Macmillan, 1972.

Harper, M. S. and R. B. Stepto. ed. *Chant of Saints.* Urbana: University of Illinois Press, 1979.

Harris, Trudier. *Black Women in the Fiction of James Baldwin.* Knoxville: University of Tennessee Press, 1985.

Hassan, Ihab. *Contemporary American Literature 1945-1972.* New York: Ungar, 1973.

Hersey, John. ed. *Ralph Ellison: A Collection of Critical Essays.* Englwood Cliffs, N.J.: Prentice-Hall, 1974.

Hill, Herbert. ed. *Anger and Beyond: The Negro Writer in the United States.* New York: Harper & Row, 1966.

Horosz, William. *The Crisis of Responsibility: Man as the Source of Accountability.* Normon: University of Oklahoma Press, 1975.

Howe, Irving. "Black Boys and Native Sons." *A World More Attractive.* New York: Horizon Press, 1963.

-----. *The Decline of the Novel.* London: Gollanz, 1971.

Jones, LeRoi. *Home: Social Essays.* New York: William Morrow, 1961.

Kaplan, Harold. *Democratic Humanism.* Chicago: University of Chicago Press, 1972.

King, M. L., Jr. *Why We Can't Wait.* New York: Harper and Row Publishers, 1963.

-----. "I Have a Dream." *Black Protest Thought in the Twentieth Century,* ed. August Meier. Indianapolis: The Bobbs Merrill Co., 1965.

Kinnamon, Keneth. *The Emergence of Richard Wright.* Chicago: University of Illinois Press, 1972.

-----. *James Baldwin: A Collection of Critical Essays.* Englewood Cliffs, N.J.: Prentice - Hall, 1974.

Klans, Gustav H. *The Socialist Novel in Britain: Towards the Recovery of a Tradition.* Brighton: The Harvester Press, 1982.

Littlejohn, David. *Black on White: A Critical Survey of Writing by American Negroes.* New York: Grossman, 1966.

Locke, Alain LeRoy. *The New Negro.* New York: Atheneum, 1968.

Macebuh, Stanley. *James Baldwin: A Critical Study.* New York: The Third Press, 1973.

Major, Clarence. *The New Black Poetry.* New York: International Publishers, 1969.

Malraux, André. *The Voices of Silence.* St. Albans, Herts.: Paladin, 1974.

Mander, John. *The Writer and Commitment.* Westport, Conn.: Greenwood Press, 1961, rpt. 1975.

Margolies, Edward. *Native Sons.* Philadelphia: J. B. Lippincott, 1968.

McSweeney, Kerry. *Invisible Man: Race and Identity.* Boston: G. K. Hall, 1988.

Moller, Karin. *The Theme of Identity in the Essays of James Baldwin: An Interpretation.* Goteborg, Sweden: Acta Universitatis Gothoburgensis, 1975.

Mphalele, Ezekiel. "African Writer and Commitment." *Voices in the Whirlwind and Other Essays.* New York: Hill and Wang, 1964.

Murray, Albert. *The Omni-Americans.* New York Outerbridge, 1970.

-----. *The Hero and the Blues.* Columbia: University of Missouri Press, 1973.

Nedal, Alan. *Invisible Criticism: Ralph Ellison and the American Canon.* Iowa City: University of Iowa Press, 1988.

Orwell, George. *The Collected Essays, Journalism and Letters*, Vol. 2. ed. Sonia Orwell and Ian Angus. Harmondsworth, Middx: Penguin Books, 1970.

O'Daniel, Therman B. *James Baldwin: A Critical Evaluation*. Washington, D.C.: Howard UP, 1981.

O'Meally, Robert G. *The Craft of Ralph Ellison*. Cambridge, Mass.: Harvard University Press, 1980.

-----. *New Essays on 'Invisible man'*. New York: Cambridge University Press, 1988.

Pratt, Louis H. *James Baldwin*. Boston: Twayne Publishers, 1978.

Quarles, Benjamin. *The Negro in the Making of America*. New York: The Macmillan Co., 1969.

Rabkin, Gerald. *Drama and Commitment*. Bloomington: Indiana University Press, 1964.

Reilly, John M. ed. *Twentieth Century Interpretations of 'Invisible Man'*. Englewood Cliffs, N.J.: Prentice-Hall, 1970.

Rosenblatt, Roger. *Black Fiction*. Cambridge, Mass.: Harvard University Press, 1974.

Ruotolo, Lucio P. *Six Existential Heroes: The Politics of Faith*. Cambridge, Mass.: Harvard University Press, 1973.

Sartre, Jean-Paul. *Existentalism and Humanism*, trans. Philip Mairet. London: Methuen Ltd., 1970.

Scott, Nathan A. *"Black Literature."* Harvard Guide to Contemporary American Writing, ed. Daniel Hoffman. Cambridge, Mass.: Harvard University Press, 1979.

Selden, Raman. *The Theory of Criticism.* London: Longman, 1988.

Shaw, Bernard. *Complete Plays with Prefaces,* Vol. III. New York: Dodd, Mead and Co., 1963.

Standley, F. L. and L. H. Pratt. *Conversations with James Baldwin.* Jackson: University of Mississippi Press, 1989.

Steiner, George. "The Writer and Communism." *Language and Silence.* New York: Atheneum, 1958, rpt. 1967.

Stepto, Robert B. *From Behind the Veil: A Study of Afro-American Narrative.* Urbana: University of Illinois Press, 1979.

Stern, J. P. *On Realism.* London: Routledge and Kegan Paul, 1973.

Sundquist, Eric J. *New Essays on 'Uncle Tom's Cabin.'* New York: Cambridge University Press, 1986.

Sylvander, Carolyn W. *James Baldwin.* New York: Ungar, 1980.

The New Columbia Encyclopedia. New York: Columbia University Press, 1975.

The Norton Anthology of American Literature, Vol. 1 and 2. New York: Norton and Co., 1989.

Tischler, N. M. *Black Masks: Negro Characters in Modern Southern Fiction.* University Park: The Pennsylvania State University Press, 1969.

Tompkins, Jane. *Sensational Designs: The Cultural Work of American Fiction 1790-1860.* New York: Oxford University Press, 1985.

Turner, David. *Black American Literature Essays.* Columbus, Ohio: Charles E. Merrill Publications Co., 1986.

Vinson, James. *20th Century Drama.* London: The Macmillan Press Ltd., 1983.

Wallace, Irving. *The Man.* New York: Bantam Books, 1974.

Weatherby, W. J. *James Baldwin: Artist on Fire - A Portrait.* New York: Donald I. Fine, 1989.

-----. *Squaring Off: Mailer Vs. Baldwin.* New York: Mason Charter, 1977.

Wells, H. G. *The Invisible man.* New York: Bantam, 1970.

Whitlow, Roger. *Black American Literature: A Critical History.* New Jersey: Little-field, Adams and Co., 1974.

Wilkinson, David. *Malraux.* Cambridge, Mass.: Harvard University Press, 1967.

Wright, Richard. *Uncle Tom's Children.* New York: Harper and Brothers, 1938.

-----. *Native Son.* New York: Harper and Row, 1940.

-----. *Twelve Million Black Voices.* New York: Viking, 1941.

-----. *Black Boy: A Record of Childhood and Youth.* New York: Harper and Brothers, 1945.

-----. *The Long Dream.* New York: Doubleday, 1958.

(b) Periodicals

Allen, Shirley S.   "Religious Symbolism and Psychic Reality in Baldwin's 'Go Tell It on the Mountain.'" *CLA Journal,* December 1975.

Baraka, Amiri. "We Carry Him as Us." *The New York Times Book Review,* 20 December 1987.

Barksdale, Richard K. "Temple of the Fire Baptized." *Phylon,* Third Quarter (1953).

Bellow, Saul. *Commentary,* 13 (June 1952).

Bigsby, C. W. E.   "The Committed Writer: James Baldwin as Dramatist." *Twentieth Century Literature,* April 1967.

Black World, 20 (December 1970); special Ellison issue.

Blake, Susan L. "Ritual and Rationalization: Black Folklore in the Works of Ralph Ellison." *PMLA,* January 1979.

Bradford, Melvin E.   "Faulkner, James Baldwin and the South," *Georgia Review,* Winter 1966.

Brathwaite, Edward. "Race and the Divided Self." *Black World,* July 1972.

Bryant, Jerry H. "Wright, Ellison, Baldwin: Exorcising the Demon." *Phylon,* June 1976.

Carson, David L. "Ralph Ellison: Twenty Years After." *Studies in American Fiction,* No. 1 (1973).

Charney, Maurice. "James Baldwin's Quarrel with Richard Wright." *American Quarterly,* Spring 1963.

Cheshire, Ardner R. "'Invisible Man' and the Life of Dialogue" *CLA Journal,* September 1977.

College Language Association Journal, 13 (1970); special Ellison issue.

Collier, Eugenia W. "Thematic Patterns in Baldwin's Essays." *Black World,* June 1972.

Cosgrove, William. "Modern Black Writers: The Divided Self." *Negro American Literature Forum,* Winter 1973.

DeMott, Benjamin. "James Baldwin on the Sixties: Acts and Revelations." *Saturday Review,* 27 May 1972.

Dickstein, Morris. "Wright, Baldwin, Cleaver." *New Letters,* XXXVIII (Winter 1971).

Featherstone, Joseph. "Blues for Mister Baldwin." *New Republic,* 27 November 1965.

Feuser, Willfried F. "Wole Soyinka: The Problem of Authenticity." *The Literary Half Yearly,* Vol. XXVIII. No. 2 (July 1987).

Fischer, R. G. "*Invisible Man* as History." *CLA Journal,* 17 (1974).

Flint, Robert W. "Not Ideas but Life: Review of *Notes of a Native Son.*" *Commentary,* May 1956.

Goldstein, Suzy B. "James Baldwin's 'Sonny's Blues': A Message in Music." *Negro American Literature Forum,* Fall 1974.

Hagopian, John V. "James Baldwin: The Black and the Red-White-and-Blue." *CLA Journal,* December 1963.

Haley, Alex. "Haley's Talk, Write, Unite." *Time,* 14 (February 1977).

Heermance, J. N. "The Modern Negro Novel." *Negro Digest,* May 1964.

Hicks, Granville. "Commitment Without Compromise." *Saturday Review,* 1 July 1961.

-----. *Saturday Review,* 24 (October 1964).

Howe, Irving. "From Harlem to Paris." *New York Times,* 26 February 1956.

-----. "James Baldwin: At Ease in Apocalypse." *Harper's,* September 1968.

Hughes, Langston. *The Nation,* Vol. 122 No. 3181 (1926).

Jacobson, Dan. "James Baldwin as Spokesman." *Commentary,* December 1961.

Jones, LeRoi. "Afro-American Literature and Class Struggle." *Black American Literature Forum,* 14:1 (1980).

Kim, Kichung. "Wright, the Protest Novel, and Baldwin's Faith." *CLA Journal,* March 1974.

Kirst, E. M. "A Langian Analysis of Blackness in Ralph Ellison's 'Invisible Man.'" *Studies in Black American Literature,* Spring, 1976.

210   R. Jothiprakash

Lewis, R. W. B. "Ellison's Essays." *New York Review of Books,* 28 January 1964.

Malcolm, Donald. "The Author in Search of Himself." *New Worker,* 25 November 1961.

Mayfield, Julian. "A Love Affair with the United States." *New Republic,* 7 August 1961.

Menand, Louis. "Liberated by Literature." *The American Review,* No. 2 (1987).

Morrison, Toni. "Life in His Language." *The New York Times Book Review,* 20 December 1987.

Nelson, E. S. "James Baldwin's Vision of Otherness and Community." *Melus,* 10, No. 2 (1983).

New York Herald Tribune Book Week, 26 (September 1965).

O'Daniel, Thermon B. "Image of Man as Portrayed by Ralph Ellison's 'Invisible Man.': *CLA Journal,* June 1967.

Pratt, Louis H. "James Baldwin and 'The Literary Ghetto.'" *CLA Journal,* December 1976.

Preston, P. "The Image: Three Views." *Opera News.* December 1962.

Reed, Ishmael. "The Essential Ellison." *Y'Bird Magazine,* Vol. 1 No. 1 (1977).

Spender, Stephen. "James Baldwin: Voice of a Revolution." *Partisan Review,* 30 (Summer 1963).

Thompson, John. "Baldwin: The Prophet as Artist." *Commentary*, June 1968.

Tischler, N. M. "Negro Literature and Classic Form." *Contemporary Literature*, Summer 1969.

Webster, H. C. "Inside a Dark Shell." *Saturday Review*, XXXV (12 April 1952).

Wright, Richard. "I Have Seen Black Hands." *New Masses*, 26 (June 1934).

-----. "Blueprint for Negro Writing." *New Masses*, 40 (5 August 1941).

-----. "I Tried to be a Communist." *Atlantic Monthly*, 174 (August 1944).

-----. *New Challenge*, II (Fall 1957).